HOOKED ON
fish

Betty Saw

To Choo Boon with love

The publisher wishes to thank **New Convox Sdn. Bhd.** for the loan and use of their tableware.

Photography: Jenhor Siow; cover photography: Joshua Tan
Cover design: Lynn Chin

Published by Marshall Cavendish Cuisine
An imprint of Marshall Cavendish International
1 New Industrial Road, Singapore 536196

Other Marshall Cavendish Offices

Marshall Cavendish Ltd. 119 Wardour Street, London W1F OUW, UK • Marshall Cavendish Corporation.
99 White Plains Road, Tarrytown NY 10591-9001, USA • Marshall Cavendish Beijing. D31A, Huatingjiayuan,
No. 6, Beisihuanzhonglu, Chaoyang District, Beijing, The People's Republic of China, 100029 • Marshall Cavendish
International (Thailand) Co Ltd. 253 Asoke, 12th Flr, Sukhumvit 21 Road, Klongtoey Nua, Wattana, Bangkok 10110,
Thailand • Marshall Cavendish (Malaysia) Sdn Bhd, Times Subang, Lot 46, Subang Hi-Tech Industrial Park, Batu Tiga,
40000 Shah Alam, Selangor Darul Ehsan, Malaysia

Marshall Cavendish is a trademark of Times Publishing Limited

National Library Board Singapore Cataloguing in Publication Data

Saw, Betty.
Hooked on fish / Betty Saw. — Singapore : Marshall Cavendish Cuisine, c2005.
p. cm.
ISBN : 981-232-961-7

1. Cookery (Fish) 1. Title.

TX747
641.692 -- dc21   SLS2005029888

Printed in Singapore by Fabulous Printers Pte Ltd

contents

acknowledgements

I would like to extend a big, heartfelt thank you to Ah Lan,
Mary Lim and Chean Harn for giving so freely their time and labour during
the photography session for this book.

preface

I am hooked on fish. It must be due to my childhood. I literally grew up on the seaside, living in a house built on stilts by the water. I remember the many hours of pleasure that this gave me and my brothers and sisters. The sea was our playground. Living by the sea and the fact that my father loved seafood meant that eating seafood was nearly an everyday affair, so it is unsurprising that I developed a liking for seafood which has remained strong until today.

I was so used to eating fresh seafood that I have become very fussy about the freshness of my seafood. Any sign of staleness, no matter how slight, would immediately put me off. I would go to great lengths, even driving long distances, to find the freshest fish possible for my table.

Only the best fish, including sea wrasse, white pomfret and exotic groupers, cooked to retain their purest form, i.e. steamed, interest me. I would delight in their delicate and smooth textures and natural sweet flavours. I have, however, learnt to like other fish from my husband. He could never appreciate steamed fish, considering it bland. He would drown it with soy sauce and smother it with chillies to suit his taste. He is not an ardent fan of fish and prefers varieties like Spanish mackerel, black pomfret and hilsa, better known as *ikan terubuk*, cooked in curries or with sauces. I have, therefore, developed numerous such recipes to ensure that fish remains a regular feature on our dining table.

We are fortunate living in the tropics to be able to enjoy such a variety of fish suitable for so many different types of recipes. I remember how limited choices were when living in the Netherlands, confined mainly to cod, salmon and sole. Once in a while, we would come across imported tropical fish in the market and would buy them immediately even though they were not that fresh.

My love for fish and the large collection of recipes that I have developed as a result prompted me to write this book and share these recipes with countless other fish lovers like me. Moreover, a diet rich in fish is recognised to be very healthy, so I hope that occasional fish eaters would also find this book helpful in adding more fish to their diets.

Happy cooking and eating fish!

— Betty Saw

baked

baked fish with percik sauce

Ingredients

Whole fish	1, about 600 g, use red snapper *(ikan merah)*, grouper *(ikan kerapu)*, threadfin *(ikan kurau/senangin)* or sultan fish *(ikan jelawat)*
Salt	1 tsp
Ground white pepper	1/4 tsp
Lemon grass *(serai)*	2 stalks, bruised
Coconut cream	250 ml, squeezed from 1/2 grated coconut with sufficient water added
Turmeric leaf *(daun kunyit)*	1, finely sliced
Kaffir lime leaves *(daun limau purut)*	4, finely sliced
Aluminium foil for wrapping fish	
Shallot oil	2–3 Tbsp
Screwpine *(pandan)* leaves	4

Ingredients to be ground (processed)

Red chillies	8, seeded
Chopped bird's eye chillies *(cili padi)*	1 tsp
Turmeric *(kunyit)*	3-cm knob, peeled
Ginger	2.5-cm knob, peeled
Lemon grass *(serai)*	2 stalks, sliced
Peeled shallots	200 g
Salt	1 1/2 tsp

Method

1. Make 2 diagonal slits across each side of fish. Season with salt and pepper and set aside.
2. Place all ingredients to be ground into a blender (processor), then blend with sufficient water added until fine.
3. Pour blended mixture into a deep saucepan. Add lemon grass and coconut cream. Cook over low heat, stirring frequently until liquid is thick.
4. Stir in turmeric and lime leaves. Remove from heat.
5. Brush aluminium foil with a little shallot oil. Place 2 screwpine leaves on top.
6. Spread 1/3 of cooked mixture onto the centre of foil piece. Place fish on top and cover with remaining mixture.
7. Drizzle on remaining shallot oil and top with remaining screwpine leaves. Wrap into a parcel.
8. With parcel in a baking tin, bake in an oven preheated to 225°C for 20 minutes.

Note: Shallot oil refers to cooking oil that has been aromatically flavoured and saved after frying raw shallot slices to a crisp.

baked fish wrapped in lotus leaf

Ingredients

Whole fish	1, 500–600 g, use red snapper *(ikan merah)* or sea bass *(ikan siakap)*
Salt	1/2 tsp
Ground white pepper	1/4 tsp
Corn flour (cornstarch)	3 rounded (heaped) tsp
Cooking oil for deep-frying	
Cooking oil	3 Tbsp
Preserved soy bean paste *(tau cheo)*	2 tsp, minced
Spring onion (scallion)	1, chopped
Bird's eye chillies *(cili padi)*	12, chopped
Lotus leaf	1, large

Shallot oil for brushing	
Aluminium foil for wrapping fish	

Ingredients to be chopped

Shallots	5, peeled
Garlic	4 cloves, peeled
Ginger	2.5-cm knob, peeled
Red chillies	2, seeded

Sauce

Plum sauce	3 Tbsp
Sugar	2 level tsp
Light soy sauce	2 tsp

Method

▌ Make 2 diagonal slits on each side of fish. Season with salt and pepper. Set aside for 15–30 minutes. Just before deep-frying, sprinkle corn flour all over fish.

▌ Deep-fry fish in hot oil for 1 minute. Drain and set aside.

▌ Heat 3 Tbsp oil in a clean saucepan. Stir-fry all chopped ingredients. When fragrant, add soy bean paste and cook for 30 seconds.

▌ Add all sauce ingredients. When liquid reaches the boil, stir in spring onion and chillies. Remove from heat.

▌ Brush lotus leaf with shallot oil, then place lotus leaf on top of foil.

▌ Spread 1/3 of cooked mixture onto lotus leaf. Place fish on top and cover with remaining mixture. Wrap into a parcel.

▌ With parcel in a baking tin or dish, bake in an oven preheated to 225°C for 15 minutes.

baked fish in tom yam sauce

Ingredients

Whole fish	1, about 600 g, use golden snapper *(ikan ungar)*, red snapper *(ikan merah)*, sea bass *(ikan siakap)*, white pomfret *(ikan bawal putih)* or grouper *(ikan kerapu)*
Salt	1/2 tsp
Ground white pepper	1/4 tsp
Cooking oil	3 Tbsp
Onion	1, peeled and diced
Tom yam paste	1 Tbsp, about 35 g
Kaffir lime leaves *(daun limau purut)*	3, finely sliced
Bird's eye chillies *(cili padi)*	10–12, sliced
Aluminium foil for wrapping fish	

Ingredients to be ground (processed)

Shallots	3, peeled
Garlic	2 cloves, peeled
Lemon grass *(serai)*	2 stalks, sliced
Galangal *(lengkuas)*	2-cm knob, peeled
Young ginger	2-cm knob, peeled
Red chillies	3–4, seeded
Dried prawn (shrimp) paste *(belacan)*	2-cm cube piece

Sauce (combined)

Water	4 Tbsp
Fish sauce	1/2 Tbsp
Lime *(limau nipis)* juice	1 Tbsp
Salt	1/2 tsp
Sugar	2 tsp

Method

▌ On each side of fish, make 2 diagonal slits across body. Season with salt and pepper and set aside.

▌ Heat oil in a saucepan or wok. Lightly brown onion pieces. Add ground ingredients and cook over low heat for 8 minutes or until fragrant.

▌ Stir in *tom yam* paste. Pour in combined sauce ingredients. Lastly, stir in lime leaves and chillies; reserve some for garnishing if desired.

▌ Cut and spread out a piece of aluminium foil large enough to wrap fish. Place fish on foil and cover with *tom yam* sauce. Wrap to seal fish.

▌ Bake foil parcel in an oven preheated to 250°C for 20 minutes.

▌ Garnish and serve.

Note: For 1.2 kg fish, double ingredient quantities in recipe and bake for 40–45 minutes.

baked fish in banana leaf

Ingredients

Whole fish	1, about 600 g, cleaned, use black pomfret *(ikan bawal hitam)* or sea bass *(ikan siakap)*
Salt	1 tsp
Ground white pepper	1/4 tsp
Sunflower oil	3 Tbsp
Kalamansi lime *(limau kesturi)* juice	1 Tbsp
Dark soy sauce	1 Tbsp
Banana leaves	1–2, greased with a little cooking oil
Bamboo toothpicks or cocktail sticks	
Red chilli	1, seeded and julienned, for garnishing
Sweet basil leaves *(daun selasih)* for garnishing	

Ingredients to be ground (processed)

Red chillies	5, seeded
Candlenuts *(buah keras)*	5
Shallots	10, peeled
Lemon grass *(serai)*	2 stalks, sliced
Dried prawn (shrimp) paste *(belacan)* granules	2 tsp
Chilli powder	1 tsp
Kaffir lime leaves *(daun limau purut)*	2
Salt	1 tsp
Sugar	1 1/2 tsp

Method

I With knife held at an angle, make 2 diagonal cuts on each side of fish. Season with salt and pepper. Set aside.

I Heat oil in a wok. Stir-fry ground ingredients over low heat until aromatic, takes 5–7 minutes.

I Stir in lime juice and soy sauce. Transfer to a small bowl and leave for a while to cool.

I Spread fried ground ingredients over fish, smearing into slits and stomach cavity.

I Wrap fish with banana leaves and secure tightly with bamboo toothpicks or cocktail sticks.

I Bake in an oven preheated to 175°C for 15–20 minutes.

I Garnish and serve hot with rice.

Note: For variation, this dish can be prepared with golden trevally (ikan gerong-gerong) or threadfin trevally (ikan cermin).

packet otak-otak

Ingredients

Cooking oil	120 ml
Spanish mackerel (ikan tenggiri) flesh	860 g, scraped from 2 large, skinned fish
Water	250 ml, mixed with 1 tsp salt
Pure coconut cream (pati santan)	250 ml
Eggs	3, large, beaten
Banana leaves	30, each 12 x 14 cm
Aluminium foil sheets	30, each 15 x 18 cm
Cooking oil for greasing	
Red chilli	1, sliced, for garnishing

Ingredients to be ground (processed)

Dried chillies	15, soaked
Lemon grass (serai)	4 stalks, sliced
Torch ginger bud (bunga kantan)	1
Galangal (lengkuas)	2.5-cm knob, peeled
Turmeric (kunyit)	15-cm knob, peeled
Candlenuts (buah keras)	15
Shallots	250 g, peeled
Garlic	5 cloves, peeled
Dried prawn (shrimp) paste (belacan)	5 x 5 x 1-cm piece
Salt	1 rounded (heaped) tsp
Sugar	5 dsp

Method

▮ Heat oil in a wok. Stir-fry ground ingredients until fragrant. Remove and set aside to cool.

▮ Place fish flesh into a blender (processor) fitted with a cutting blade. Blend until pasty. Transfer to a mixing bowl.

▮ Gradually mix in salted water, then add cooled fried paste and coconut cream. Mix well. Lastly, add beaten eggs and mix until thoroughly combined.

▮ To wrap, place a piece of banana leaf over a piece of foil. Lightly grease banana leaf surface with cooking oil.

▮ Place 4 tsp fish paste onto the centre of banana leaf. Fold into a packet and seal all the edges.

▮ Use hands to flatten foil packet and to level out filling, producing a neat rectangular package. Repeat wrapping process until fish paste is used up.

▮ Place packets on a baking tray. Bake in an oven preheated to 200°C for 15 minutes.

▮ To serve, open packets and garnish as desired.

tuna and egg pie

Ingredients

Puff pastry	1 kg, see pg 26 for recipe
Egg white	1, beaten, or 1 egg yolk mixed with 2 tsp milk
Filling*	1 recipe, see below
Hard-boiled eggs	3, shelled and quartered

Method

I Divide pastry into 2 parts; one part is slightly more than half. The bigger part is for the base and the smaller for the top.

I On a lightly floured surface, roll out bigger part into a circle about 34 cm in diameter. Then, line a 30-cm pizza tray. Pastry will form a 2–2.5-cm border outside of tray for folding later. Brush edges with beaten egg white.

I Spoon filling onto pastry centre and spread out evenly. Press hard-boiled egg quarters into filling.

I On a lightly floured surface, roll out smaller part of dough into a circle about 30 cm in diameter. Lightly score pastry with curving lines from centre without cutting through. Carefully turn over and brush edges with egg white.

I Place pastry, patterned side up, over filling. Pleat bottom piece edges over those of top piece to seal.

I Re-roll remaining pastry. With cookie cutters, make heart-shaped and round fluted pieces and use to decorate pie.

I Brush top of pie with remaining beaten egg white. Make a few slits, cutting right through pastry to allow steam to escape.

I Bake in an oven preheated to 220°C for 35 minutes or until golden brown.

*Filling

Cooking oil	1 Tbsp	Sugar	1 tsp
Onion	1, peeled and thinly sliced	Canned button mushrooms	1 can (425 g), drained and quartered
Canned tuna (ikan tongkol) chunks in oil	2 cans (185 g), drained	Red capsicum (bell pepper)	1, small, diced
Worcestershire sauce	1 tsp	Red chillies	2, seeded and sliced
Salt	2 tsp	Frozen green peas	150 g
Ground white pepper	1 tsp	Mustard sauce**	1 recipe, see opposite

Method

▌ Heat oil in a saucepan and fry onion slices until softened. Add tuna chunks, Worcestershire sauce, salt, pepper and sugar. Stir in mushrooms, capsicum, chillies and peas.

▌ Fold all ingredients into prepared mustard sauce, then transfer a deep dish to cool.

**Mustard Sauce

Butter	50 g	Ground white	
Plain (all purpose)		pepper	1/4 tsp
flour	50 g	Chopped parsley	1 Tbsp
UHT milk	600 ml	Chopped coriander	
Mild prepared		leaves (cilantro)	1 Tbsp
mustard	1/2 Tbsp	Chopped spring	
Salt	1/2 tsp	onion (scallion)	1 Tbsp

Method

▌ Melt butter in a non-stick pan. Add flour and gently cook mixture, stirring until it comes away from sides of the pan. Gradually mix in milk, stirring well to avoid lumps.

▌ Once all the milk is added, swap wooden spoon for a balloon whisk. Over medium heat, whisk continuously until sauce is thick and smooth. Simmer gently for 1–2 minutes, stirring until thickened.

▌ Add mustard, salt, pepper and fresh herbs. Set aside.

Note: Instead of 1 large pie, make 2 smaller ones. First, divide pastry into 2 parts. Roll out 1 part into a large rectangle, about 0.5-cm thick. Cut out a circle 28 cm in diameter to fit a 28-cm pizza tray. Re-roll remaining pastry and cut a circle 22 cm in diameter tracing a 22-cm pie pan. Proceed to make pie as described for large pie. Repeat with remaining part of pastry to make second pie.

baked threadfin with onion sauce

Ingredients

Threadfin (*ikan kurau/senangin*)	1 whole, about 1 kg, cleaned
Salt	3 tsp
Sugar	1 tsp
Ground white pepper	1/4 tsp
Cooking oil for deep-frying	
Cooking oil	1 Tbsp
Onion	1, peeled and shredded
Red chilli	1, seeded and coarsely chopped
Corn flour (cornstarch)	1/2 Tbsp, mixed with 1 Tbsp water to make thickener
Spring onions (scallions)	2, chopped
Coriander leaves (cilantro)	3 sprigs, chopped
Red chilli	1, seeded and julienned, for garnishing

Ingredients to be combined

Egg	1, beaten
Corn flour (cornstarch)	2 Tbsp
Plain (all-purpose) flour	2 Tbsp

Sauce (combined)

Chicken stock	225 ml
Worcestershire sauce	1 1/2 Tbsp
A1 sauce	1 Tbsp
Sugar	1 Tbsp
Light soy sauce	1 Tbsp
Sesame oil	1 tsp
Salt	1/4 tsp

Method

▌ Make 3 diagonal slits on each side of fish. Season with salt, sugar and pepper. Set aside for at least 15 minutes. Just before deep-frying, coat fish with combined ingredients.

▌ Heat sufficient oil for deep-frying. Cook prepared fish in hot oil for about 1 minute. Drain.

▌ Transfer fried fish to a heatproof (flameproof) serving dish. Bake in an oven preheated to 220°C for 15–20 minutes.

▌ Meanwhile, heat 1 Tbsp oil in a clean wok. Stir-fry onion, then chilli. Pour in combined sauce ingredients. Stir in gravy from heatproof dish and simmer for 30 seconds.

▌ Add thickener, then stir in spring onions and coriander leaves; reserve some for garnishing if desired. Pour sauce over fish, garnish and serve.

salmon with creamy mushrooms

Ingredients

Salmon (ikan salmon)	4 steaks or 6 fillets, about 450 g	Fresh shiitake, button or oyster mushrooms	225 g, quartered
Aluminium foil for lining baking tray		Chicken stock	3 Tbsp
Cooking oil	1 Tbsp	Crème fraîche or double (heavy whipping) cream	200 ml
Salt	to taste	Salt	1/2 tsp
Ground white pepper	to taste	Ground black pepper	1/2 tsp
Fresh chives or parsley for garnishing		Corn flour (cornstarch)	1 tsp, mixed with 2 Tbsp chicken stock to make thickener

Sauce

Olive oil	1 1/2 Tbsp	Chopped parsley	1 Tbsp
Onions	125 g, peeled and diced	Chopped Chinese (garlic) chives	2 Tbsp
Garlic	3 cloves, peeled and crushed	Lemon juice	1 Tbsp

Method

▌ Prepare sauce. Heat olive oil in a frying pan. Add onions and garlic and cook, stirring, for about 5 minutes.

▌ Add mushrooms and cook for 3–4 minutes, stirring frequently. Add chicken stock and bring to the boil.

▌ Add cream, salt and black pepper. Allow to boil gently for 1–2 minutes. Stir in thickener, then remove from heat. Set aside.

▌ Place salmon on a foil-lined baking tray. Brush with cooking oil and season to taste with salt and pepper. Cook under a medium grill for 3–4 minutes or until just cooked.

▌ Meanwhile, add parsley, chives and lemon juice to sauce and return to the boil.

▌ Arrange salmon on serving plates. Spoon mushroom sauce over. Garnish and serve.

Note: Crème fraîche is a naturally fermented thick cream, with hints of nuttiness and tanginess in its flavour.

salmon cream pie

Ingredients

Shortcrust (pie) pastry*	240 g, see recipe below
Double (heavy whipping) cream	150 ml
Eggs	3, large, beaten
Cooked flaked fish fillet	150 g, use salmon (ikan salmon), threadfin (ikan kurau/senangin) or grouper (ikan kerapu)
Lemon juice	2 tsp
Hot prepared mustard	1 tsp
Worcestershire sauce	1 tsp
Red or green capsicum (bell pepper)	1/2, diced into 0.75-cm pieces
Ground white pepper	1/2 tsp
Salt	1/2 tsp or to taste
Paprika	1/4 tsp

Ingredients to be chopped

Parsely	a few sprigs
Spring onion (scallion)	1
Coriander leaves (cilantro)	2 sprigs

Method

I In between 2 plastic sheets, roll out pastry into 0.4-cm thickness, then line a 23–25-cm springform, or false-bottomed, pie tin. Prick base with a fork. Refrigerate for 15–20 minutes.

I Bake blind, or pastry without filling, in an oven preheated to 190°C until light golden, takes 15–20 minutes.

I To make filling, first beat cream and beaten eggs together. Then, add all remaining ingredients, including chopped ingredients, and mix well.

I Pour filling onto cooled pastry case. Bake for 35 minutes or until filling is set and golden.

*Shortcrust pastry

Self-raising flour	225 g
Salt	a pinch
Cold butter	135 g, diced
Cold water	60 ml

Method

I Sift flour into bowl of a blender (processor) and add salt and butter. Blend until mixture is crumbly. Drizzle in water and 'pulse' the mixture until a crumbly ball of dough forms.

I Remove dough from blender and lightly shape into a soft ball. Place into a plastic bag lightly dusted with some extra flour. Refrigerate bagged dough for 30 minutes before using.

Note: Prepared mustard refers to dry or powdered mustard that has been mixed with other ingredients and seasonings to take a liquid form, usually of spreading consistency.

salmon encased in puff pastry

Ingredients

Salmon (ikan salmon) steaks	2, deboned and skinned	Sugar	1/2 tsp
Salt	1/2 tsp	Ground white pepper	1/4 tsp
Freshly ground black pepper	to taste	French or dijon mustard	1 tsp
Puff pastry*	350 g, see recipe below	Grated lemon rind	1/2 tsp
Egg white	1/2	Chopped spring onion (scallion), parsley or dill	1 Tbsp
Sesame seeds		Tomatoes	3, medium-sized, peeled and chopped
Mayonnaise (combined)		Onion	1/2, peeled and chopped
Mayonnaise	3 Tbsp		
Salt	1/2 tsp		

Method

I Season salmon steaks with salt and pepper. Heat a dry frying pan. Sear steaks on both sides, about 1 minute.

I Halve pastry. Roll out each part into a 20 × 30-cm rectangle. Brush with egg white.

I Place salmon on 1 pastry rectangle. Spoon mayonnaise onto the centre of each steak.

I Make a few slits on other piece of pastry and place on top of mayonnaise to cover steaks.

I Press and crimp edges of pastry to seal completely. Brush with egg white and sprinkle on sesame seeds.

I Bake in an oven preheated to 220°C for 20 minutes or until golden.

*Puff Pastry

Pastry margarine	180 g, at room temperature	**Ingredients to be combined**	
Plain (all-purpose) flour	480 g	Kalamansi lime (limau kesturi) juice	extracted from 2 small limes
Baking powder	1 1/2 tsp	Cold water	175 ml
Corn oil	85 ml	Salt	1/4 tsp
Egg	1, beaten		

Method

| In between large plastic sheets, roll out pastry margarine into a 15 x 20-cm rectangle. Refrigerate.

| Sift flour and baking powder into a mixing bowl. Add corn oil and beaten egg. Blend with a pastry cutter until mixture resembles breadcrumbs. Bind with combined ingredients to form soft dough.

| On a lightly floured board, knead dough until smooth. Cover dough and leave to rest for 15–30 minutes.

| Roll out rested dough into a rectangle twice as long as margarine rectangle but of the same width, or 30 x 20 cm.

| Place pastry margarine on centre of rolled out dough. Fold in ends of dough to cover margarine. Seal edges.

| Roll out parcel to a rectangle twice as long as it is wide. Fold into thirds lengthways. Repeat rolling and folding process twice.

| Halve pastry for easier handling and use as required.

baked lemak fish in foil

Ingredients

Spanish mackerel (ikan tenggiri)	2 slices, each about 200 g
Aluminium foil for wrapping fish	
Cooking oil for brushing	
Screwpine (pandan) leaves	4

Ingredients to be ground (processed)

Dried chillies	10
Turmeric (kunyit)	2.5-cm knob, peeled
Young galangal (lengkuas)	3-cm knob, peeled
Dried prawn (shrimp) paste (belacan)	1 x 2 x 2-cm piece
Candlenuts (buah keras)	4
Lemon grass (serai)	2 stalks, sliced
Pure coconut cream (pati santan)	125 ml, squeezed from 1/2 grated coconut
Cooking oil	1 Tbsp
Salt	1 tsp
Sugar	1/2 tsp

Method

| Marinate fish slices with ground ingredients for at least 1 hour. Refrigerate until cooking time.

| Grease foil with cooking oil. Place screwpine leaves along the centre, then fish on top. Cover with ground ingredients. Fold foil over and seal 3 edges securely.

| Oven toast (preheated) for about 12 minutes.

vietnamese baked fish with ginger and mushroom sauce

Ingredients

Whole fish	1, 600–800 g, use sea bass *(ikan siakap)*, red snapper *(ikan merah)*, grouper *(ikan kerapu)* or carp *(ikan tongsan)*
Cooking oil	2 Tbsp
Garlic	2 cloves, peeled and chopped
Dried Chinese mushrooms	3, soaked, stems discarded and sliced
Lemon grass *(serai)*	2 stalks, thinly sliced
Young ginger	3-cm knob, peeled and finely shredded
Red chilli	1, seeded and cut into strips
Potato flour	1/2 Tbsp, mixed with 3 Tbsp stock to make thickener

Seasoning (combined)

Chopped dill	1 Tbsp
Sesame oil	1 Tbsp
Shallot oil	1 Tbsp
Salt	1 tsp
Ground white pepper	1 tsp

Sauce (combined)

Ginger wine	90 ml
Fish sauce	1 Tbsp
Light soy sauce	1 Tbsp
Salt	1 tsp
Sugar	1/2 tsp
Chicken stock	250 ml
Wine vinegar	2 Tbsp

Method

I Gut and clean fish. Make 2 diagonal slits on each side of fish. Season with combined seasoning ingredients and set aside.

I Bake fish in an oven preheated to 200°C for 35–40 minutes.

I Heat oil in a wok. Stir-fry garlic, mushrooms, lemon grass and ginger until fragrant. Pour in combined sauce ingredients and bring to the boil.

I Reduce heat and simmer for 5 minutes. Stir in red chilli and thickener.

I Pour over hot baked fish.

Note: For Muslims, use any type of rice vinegar instead of wine vinegar.

braised

braised fish head

Ingredients

Song fish head *(ikan tongsan kepala besar)*	1.3 kg, washed and cleaned
Chinese cooking wine *(hua tiao)*	1 Tbsp
Light soy sauce	2 Tbsp
Ground white pepper	1/2 tsp
Cooking oil for deep-frying	
Chicken breast or thigh fillets	150 g, skinned if desired and diagonally sliced
Light soy sauce	1/2 tsp
Corn flour (cornstarch)	1 tsp
Egg white	1
Cooking oil	2 Tbsp
Ginger	6 slices, peeled
Spring onion (scallion)	1, cut into 6-cm lengths
Prepared Chinese mushrooms*	1 recipe, see opposite
Chinese cabbage	500 g, halve each leaf then cut each half into 3 pieces

Ground white pepper	a dash
Chinese cooking wine *(hua tiao)*	1 Tbsp
Corn flour (cornstarch)	2 tsp, mixed with 2 Tbsp water to make thickener
Sesame oil	2 tsp

Sauce (combined)

Light soy sauce	2 Tbsp
Sugar	3 tsp
Dark soy sauce	1/2 tsp
Ground white pepper	a dash
Chicken stock	500 ml

Garnishing

Shredded spring onion (scallion)

Shredded coriander leaves (cilantro)

Method

I Split fish head into 2 without cutting through. Pierce eyes with a sharp, pointed knife to prevent oil-splatter when deep-frying later. Season fish head with 1 Tbsp wine, 2 Tbsp light soy sauce and 1/2 tsp pepper.

I Heat sufficient oil for deep-frying in a wok. Deep-fry fish head until 80 per cent cooked. Drain and set aside.

I Season chicken slices with 1/2 tsp light soy sauce, 1 tsp corn flour and egg white.

I Heat 2 Tbsp oil in a clean wok. Stir-fry ginger and spring onion. Add chicken and toss for 30 seconds, then add prepared mushrooms and cabbage. Stir-fry for 1 minute.

I Add fish head to wok, skin-side down. Pour in combined sauce ingredients and add a dash pepper. Cover wok and simmer over medium heat for 3 minutes.

I Remove cover and drizzle in 1 Tbsp wine. Add thickener and drizzle in sesame oil.

I Garnish and serve.

*Prepared Chinese mushrooms

Dried Chinese mushrooms	10, stems discarded
Corn flour (cornstarch)	3 tsp
Cooking oil or chicken fat	1 Tbsp
Ginger	1 thick slice
Spring onion (scallion)	1, white part only, lightly smashed

Sauce (combined)

Oyster sauce	2 Tbsp
Light soy sauce	1 Tbsp
Sugar	2 tsp
Chicken stock	375 ml

Method

▮ Soak mushrooms in some water. Drain and rub with corn flour. Wash under running tap, twice.

▮ Bring a saucepan of water to the boil. Add mushrooms and boil for 5 minutes. Rinse and drain boiled mushrooms.

▮ Heat oil or preferably chicken fat in a non-stick wok. Fry ginger and spring onion, then add mushrooms and toss for 30 seconds.

▮ Pour in combined sauce ingredients and bring to the boil.

▮ Cover and simmer over very low heat for 45–50 minutes.

Note: For Muslims, the Chinese rice wine in this recipe can be omitted without seriously affecting the overall taste of the dish.

braised fish with mushrooms

Ingredients

Fish fillet	500 g, cut into 0.75-cm thick slices, use grouper *(ikan kerapu)* or red snapper *(ikan merah)*
Corn flour (cornstarch)	1 rounded (heaped) Tbsp
Cooking oil for deep-frying	
Cooking oil	1½ Tbsp
Ginger	3 thick slices, peeled
Minced garlic	1 Tbsp
Dried Chinese mushrooms	6, soaked to soften and stems discarded
Canned straw mushrooms	10–12, halved
Fresh chicken stock	375 ml
Red chilli	1, seeded and shredded
Spring onions (scallions)	3, cut into 3-cm lengths

Seasoning

Salt	1 tsp
Sugar	1 tsp
Sesame oil	1 tsp

Sauce (combined)

Oyster sauce	1 Tbsp
Dark soy sauce	1 tsp
Sugar	1 tsp
Salt	¼ tsp
Ground white pepper	¼ tsp
Chinese rice wine	1 tsp

Thickener (combined)

Corn flour (cornstarch)	½ Tbsp
Stock or water	1 Tbsp

Method

▌ Season fish with seasoning ingredients. Leave for 15 minutes. Just before deep-frying, coat fish with corn flour.

▌ Heat sufficient oil for deep-frying until hot. Deep-fry fish until crisp and cooked through. Drain and set aside.

▌ Heat 1½ Tbsp oil in a clean wok. Lightly brown ginger and garlic. Add mushrooms and stir-fry for 1 minute.

▌ Add fish to wok, then chicken stock. Cover and cook over medium-low heat for 7 minutes.

▌ Stir in combined sauce ingredients and thickener, then lastly, chilli and spring onions. Dish out and serve.

indonesian hot and sour fish soup

Ingredients

Fish fillets	250 g, use garfish (*ikan todak*), tuna (*ikan tongkol*) or eel (*ikan belut*)	Bird's eye chillies (*cili padi*)	5, left whole
Salt	I tsp	Ground dried chillies	2 tsp
Ground white pepper	1/4 tsp	Ginger	2-cm knob, peeled and crushed
Lime (*limau nipis*) juice	I Tbsp	Chicken stock	400 ml
		Fish sauce	I 1/2 Tbsp
Cooking oil	I Tbsp	Kaffir lime leaves (*daun limau purut*)	4, finely sliced
Garlic	3 cloves, finely chopped		
Lemon grass (*serai*)	2 stalks, crushed	Salt	to taste

Method

I If using garfish or tuna, cut into 5-cm cubes or desired serving size. If using eel, cut into 3-cm wide pieces. Wash and drain.

I Season fish pieces with salt, pepper and lime juice. Set aside.

I Heat oil in a medium-sized saucepan. Stir-fry garlic and lemon grass. Add bird's eye chillies, ground dried chillies and ginger. Cook for I minute.

I Pour in chicken stock and bring to the boil. Add fish sauce and fish pieces. Allow to boil over medium-low heat for 5 minutes.

I Sprinkle in kaffir lime leaves; reserve some for garnishing if desired. Adjust to taste with salt and serve.

Note: Cuttlefish and prawns can be used instead of fish.

clay pot seafood porridge

Ingredients

Threadfin (ikan kurau/ senangin) fillet or steak	250 g, cut into 5 x 1-cm pieces	Young ginger	20 g, peeled and shredded
Salt	1/2 tsp	Garlic	1 clove, peeled, smashed and minced
Ground white pepper	1/2 tsp	Ground white pepper	1/4 tsp
Prawns (shrimps)	300 g, medium–large	Light soy sauce	1/2 Tbsp
Rice	100 g	Sesame oil	1 tsp or more to taste
Water	1.5 litres	Spring onions (scallions)	2, chopped
Salt	1 1/4 tsp		

Method

I Season fish with 1/2 tsp salt and 1/2 tsp pepper. Set aside.

I Trim off feelers and eyes of cleaned prawns but leave unpeeled. Slit open backs of prawns to devein.

I Put rice together with water and 1 1/4 tsp salt in a large clay pot. Cover and bring to the boil over high heat, about 12 minutes.

I Remove cover and stir to prevent sticking. Reduce heat and simmer, uncovered, for 15 minutes.

I Stir in ginger, garlic and 1/4 tsp pepper. Continue to simmer for another 15 minutes.

I Stir in soy sauce and sesame oil. Increase heat to high and add fish and prawns.

I Cover and bring to the boil. Simmer for 2 minutes, then turn off heat. Keep covered for 3 minutes before serving.

I Serve porridge sprinkled with sesame oil and spring onions.

salted fresh fish, oyster and tangerine peel porridge

Ingredients

White fish fillet or steak	250 g, use grouper (ikan kerapu), white pomfret (ikan bawal putih) or threadfin (ikan kurau/senangin)
Coarse sea salt	1½ Tbsp
Rice	150 g (1 rice cup)
Salt	1 tsp
Shallot oil	2 tsp
Water	2 litres
Shallot or cooking oil	1 tsp
Young ginger	2.5-cm knob, peeled and finely shredded
Dried oysters	4, large, each 15–18g, soaked for 10 minutes
Century egg	1, shelled and quartered
Dried tangerine peel	3 g, soaked for 15 minutes, pith scraped with a teaspoon and chopped
Dried scallops	2, large, rinsed, soaked in 60 ml water and shredded

Garnishing

Chinese cruellers (yau char kwai)	6, snipped into 1-cm thick pieces
Spring onions (scallions)	2, thinly sliced

Method

▌ Prepare salted fresh fish. Wipe fish with a clean damp tea towel (do not rinse), then rub both sides with coarse salt. Transfer salted fish to a covered container and refrigerate for 2 days.

▌ On cooking day, rinse salted fish under a running tap to rid salt, then drain and cut into 4 x 0.5-cm pieces. Set aside.

▌ Put washed rice into an electric rice cooker. Rub rice with salt and 2 tsp shallot oil. Set aside for 15 minutes.

▌ Heat 1 tsp oil in a small non-stick saucepan and lightly brown ginger and oysters. Remove and add to rice cooker.

▌ Add in remaining ingredients, including the soaking liquid for scallops, and switch appliance on to rice cooking mode.

▌ When rice mixture reaches the boil, takes 15–20 minutes, switch appliance to porridge mode. Leave to cook for 1 hour 30 minutes or until gooey and thick.

▌ Stir in fish slices and allow to cook for 5 minutes more. Garnish and serve.

Note: Dried tangerine peel is the sun-dried peel of Chinese tangerines, or Mandarin oranges. If well dried, the peel can store indefinitely in an airtight tin can in a cool place. Do not store in the refrigerator as the dampness causes loss of flavour. Generally, the more mature the peel, the higher its nutritional value and, therefore, its cost. The best ones are reputedly 20–30 years old. They are valued for their subtle fragrance and for their herbal properties in curing loss of appetite, flatulence, diarrhoea, vomiting and coughs. Dried tangerine peel is an essential ingredient in the Chinese dessert Red Bean Pudding (Hoong Tau Sar) and in Cantonese-style rice porridge dishes, especially those involving meat.

catfish and black bean soup

Ingredients

Catfish (ikan sembilang/keli)	600 g
Black beans	300 g
Water	2 litres
Salt	1 tsp or more to taste
Cooking oil	1 Tbsp
Old ginger	2.5-cm knob, peeled, halved and lightly smashed

Method

❙ Gut and clean catfish, then cut into 5-cm pieces. Set aside.

❙ Put black beans into a clean wok and dry fry over medium-low heat for 5 minutes or until fragrant.

❙ Pour in sufficient water to cover black beans. Bring to the boil and simmer for 2–3 minutes. Drain black beans and transfer to a deep saucepan. Discard blackish liquid.

❙ Add 2 litres water and salt to black beans. Bring to the boil, then reduce heat and simmer for 30 minutes.

❙ Meanwhile, heat oil a non-stick wok and lightly brown ginger. Dish out and add to simmering black beans.

❙ In the same wok, fry catfish for 1–2 minutes, then remove and add to black beans in saucepan.

❙ When liquid returns to the boil, reduce heat to low and simmer for 15 minutes. Adjust to taste with more salt if necessary.

❙ Serve hot with rice.

Note: This tasty soup is deeply aromatic with a distinctive nuttiness and according to principles in traditional Chinese medicine (TCM), it also helps to expel heat and is, thus, beneficial to people who suffer from nose bleeds, which are believed to be caused by excessive heat or heatiness in the bodily system. This soup is also ideal for backache sufferers because TCM practitioners commonly recommend the consumption of black beans to treat the condition.

nyonya asam fish soup

Ingredients

Whole baby threadfin (ikan kurau/senangin)	600 g, or 5–6 mullets (ikan belanak), each 100–120 g	Red chillies	2, large, halved lengthways, seeded and diagonally sliced into 0.5-cm slices
Salt	1 tsp	Bird's eye chillies (cili padi)	2, halved lengthways
Tamarind pulp (asam Jawa)	30 g, mixed with 250 ml water and strained	Lemon grass (serai)	4 stalks, diagonally sliced into 0.5-cm slices
Chicken stock	560 ml	Sugar	4 tsp
Dried prawn (shrimp) paste (belacan)	20 g, dissolved in 2 Tbsp water	Salt	1 tsp or more to taste
		Tomato	1, large, cut into 6 wedges
Onion	1, peeled and cut into 8 wedges	Fresh shiitake mushrooms	2, quartered
		Kalamansi lime (limau kesturi) juice	extracted from 1 lime

Method

▌ Season fish with 1 tsp salt. Leave for 10 minutes.

▌ Combine tamarind juice and chicken stock in a medium cooking pot. Bring to the boil.

▌ Add dried prawn paste solution, onion, both chillies and lemon grass. Cover and allow to simmer for 5 minutes or until onions are soft.

▌ Stir in sugar and salt to taste, then add tomato and simmer for 1 minute. Add fish and mushrooms and simmer for 4–5 minutes.

▌ Lastly, stir in lime juice. Serve hot with rice.

Note: Fragrant and tangy, this oil-free soup is quick and easy to prepare.

braised eel with bamboo shoots

Ingredients

Eel *(ikan belut)*	600 g
Salt	2 tsp
Sesame oil	1 tsp
Ground white pepper	$1/2$ tsp
Cooking oil	4 Tbsp
Dried Chinese mushrooms	4, soaked to soften, stems discarded and quartered
Bamboo shoots	90 g, sliced
Garlic	2 cloves, peeled and sliced
Shallots	2, peeled and sliced
Ginger	4-cm knob, peeled and shredded
Chinese rice wine	2 tsp
Spring onions (scallions)	3, cut into 2.5-cm lengths
Red chillies	2, seeded and julienned

Corn flour (cornstarch)	2 rounded (heaped) tsp, mixed with 1 Tbsp water
Sesame oil	$1/2$ tsp
Chinese black vinegar	$1/2$ tsp

Sauce (combined)

Fresh anchovy *(ikan bilis)* or chicken stock	375 ml
Light soy sauce	1 Tbsp
Thick dark soy sauce	1 tsp
Sesame oil	$1/2$ tsp
Sugar	1 tsp
Salt	$1/2$ tsp
Ground white pepper	$1/2$ tsp

Method

▌ Clean eel after removing head and tail. Blanch in boiling water for 1 minute. Drain and allow to cool slightly.

▌ Rub eel with some salt to remove slime on the skin. Rinse well with cold water. Debone eel and cut into 4-cm pieces. Season with salt, sesame oil and pepper.

▌ Heat 2 Tbsp oil in a wok. Add mushrooms and stir-fry for 1 minute. Add bamboo shoots and stir-fry for another minute. Remove and set aside.

▌ Reheat wok with remaining oil and lightly brown garlic, shallots and ginger. Add eel pieces and stir-fry gently for 1 minute.

▌ Add rice wine and stir briskly. Return mushrooms and bamboo shoots to wok, then pour in combined sauce ingredients.

▌ Bring to the boil, reduce heat and simmer for 8–10 minutes or until eel is tender.

▌ Add spring onions and chillies, then corn flour solution to thicken.

▌ Stir in sesame oil and vinegar. Dish out and serve.

Note: For Muslims, the Chinese rice wine in this recipe can be omitted without seriously affecting the overall taste of the dish.

curried

asam fish head

Ingredients

Fish head	1, large, about 1.5–2 kg, cut into large pieces, use grouper (ikan kerapu) or red snapper (ikan merah)
Salt	1 tsp
Ground white pepper	1/2 tsp
Cooking oil	1 Tbsp
Lemon grass (serai)	4 stalks, smashed
Torch ginger buds (bunga kantan)	3, 1 sliced and 2 split
Onion	1, peeled and quartered
Tamarind pulp (asam Jawa)	2 Tbsp
Water	1 litre
Sugar	1 Tbsp
Salt	1 1/2 tsp
Tomatoes	2, quartered
Polygonum leaves (daun kesum)	15 sprigs, stems discarded

Ingredients to be ground (processed)

Fresh red chillies	10, or 15 dried chillies
Shallots	14–15, peeled
Dried prawn (shrimp) paste (belacan)	2.5-cm cube piece
Turmeric (kunyit)	2.5-cm knob, peeled

Method

▌ Season fish head pieces with 1 tsp salt and 1/2 tsp pepper.

▌ Heat oil in a wok and lightly sauté ground ingredients.

▌ Except fish head, tomatoes and polygonum leaves, combine all other ingredients, including those sautéed, in a large pot. Bring to a slow boil, then reduce heat and simmer for 15 minutes.

▌ Add remaining ingredients. Simmer for 10 minutes more or until fish head is cooked.

Note: For Lemak Asam Fish Head, stir in 125 ml coconut cream when fish head is just cooked. Also, polygonum leaves are sometimes known as laksa leaves or Vietnamese mint.

fish red curry

Ingredients

Sunflower oil	2 Tbsp	Red chillies	2, halved lengthways
Thai-style red curry paste*	4½ Tbsp, see recipe below	Fresh green peppercorns	1 Tbsp
Fish sauce	3 Tbsp	Red snapper (ikan merah) or sea bass	
Sugar	1 tsp	(ikan siakap)	600 g, sliced into 2.5-cm thick pieces
Dried anchovy (ikan bilis) stock	565 ml, or water	Kaffir lime leaves (daun limau purut)	5, split
Long (snake) beans	150 g, cut into 2.5-cm lengths	Bird's eye chillies (cili padi) (optional)	6–8
Small aubergines (eggplants/brinjals)	150 g, quartered	Holy basil	35 g

Method

▌ Heat oil in a deep saucepan and add curry paste. Cook for 2–3 minutes.

▌ Add fish sauce, sugar and water or stock. Bring to the boil.

▌ Add long beans, aubergines, red chillies and peppercorns. Stir well and simmer for 2–3 minutes.

▌ Add fish, lime leaves, bird's eye chillies and basil. Simmer for 1 minute more or until cooked. Serve.

*Red Curry Paste

Lemon grass (serai)	3 stalks, sliced		
Galangal (lengkuas)	40 g, peeled		
Dried chillies	10, soaked and seeded		
Garlic	5–6 cloves, peeled	Kaffir lime zest	2 tsp
Dried prawn (shrimp) paste (belacan)	1 Tbsp	Coriander (cilantro) roots	2
Kaffir lime leaves (daun limau purut)	2–3	Ground white pepper	1 tsp

Method

▌ Combine ingredients in an electric blender (processor) until fine. If storing paste for future use, fry with 1 Tbsp cooking oil first.

curried

fish head curry with mixed vegetables and rice vermicelli

Ingredients

Fish head	1.5–2 kg, cut into 2.5-cm cubes, use grouper *(ikan kerapu)* or mangrove snapper *(ikan jenahak)*
Salt	1½ tsp
Ground white pepper	½ tsp
Salt	1 tsp
Sugar	1 tsp
Cooking oil	2 tsp
Long (snake) beans	300 g, cut into 5-cm lengths
Cabbage	500 g, cut into 3-cm squares
Aubergines (eggplants/brinjals)	300 g, cut into 1 x 5-cm fingers
Lady's fingers (okra)	200 g, cut diagonally into 1-cm wide slices
Bean sprouts	250 g, tailed
Fried bean curd puffs *(tau pok)*	240 g
Dried rice vermicelli	400 g, of medium thickness

Curry

Cooking oil	3 Tbsp
Curry leaves	6 sprigs, stems discarded
Fried salted fish	100 g, finely ground
Salt	3 tsp or to taste
Dried anchovy (ikan bilis) stock	4.5 litres
Pure coconut cream *(pati santan)*	400 ml

Ingredients to be ground (processed)

Shallots	600 g, peeled
Turmeric *(kunyit)*	8-cm knob, peeled
Dried chillies	30, seeded and soaked to soften
Dried prawn (shrimp) paste *(belacan)*	2 pieces, each 2 x 5 cm
Candlenuts *(buah keras)*	14
Lemon grass *(serai)*	4 stalks, sliced
Galangal *(lengkuas)*	3 x 5-cm knob, peeled

Method

1. Season fish head pieces with 1½ tsp salt and pepper. Set aside.

1. Prepare curry. Heat oil in a deep saucepan and fry ground ingredients until fragrant. Add curry leaves and stir-fry for 2 minutes, then stir in salted fish and salt to taste. Add stock and bring to the boil. Reduce heat and simmer for 5 minutes. Stir in coconut cream and bring to a slow boil over low heat. Set aside.

1. Bring a large saucepan of water to the boil with 1 tsp salt and sugar, as well as 2 tsp oil added. Separately scald vegetables and bean curd puffs. Drain well. Except bean sprouts, arrange all other scalded ingredients on a large, shallow serving dish.

1. Put dried rice vermicelli into a basin and pour in sufficient boiling water to cover. Leave to soak for 10 minutes. Drain and transfer to a large saucepan of boiling water. Allow to boil over medium heat for 7–8 minutes or until just cooked. Drain well and bathe in a basin of cool boiled water. Separate strands, drain and transfer to a serving dish. Mix in bean sprouts. Set aside until ready to serve.

1. Bring a medium saucepan of water to the boil. Lower in fish head pieces to cook for 5 minutes. Drain and set aside.

1. Just before serving, heat up curry and add in fish. Heat until liquid is just beginning to boil. Ladle curry, with fish, over prepared vegetables. Serve with rice vermicelli and bean sprouts.

fish asam pedas daun kesum

Ingredients

Spanish mackerel (ikan tenggiri)	600–800 g, cut into steaks
Salt	1/2 tsp
Ground white pepper	1/4 tsp
Cooking oil	2 Tbsp
Garlic	4 cloves, peeled and sliced
Ginger	2.5-cm knob, peeled and sliced
Tamarind pulp (asam Jawa)	45 g, mixed with 625 ml water and strained
Salt	1/2 tsp
Sugar	1 rounded (heaped) tsp
Polygonum leaves (daun kesum)	60 g

Ingredients to be ground (processed)

Red chillies	6, seeded
Chilli paste	1 rounded (heaped) Tbsp, about 50 g
Fresh turmeric (kunyit)	5-cm knob, peeled
Dried prawn (shrimp) paste (belacan) granules	4 tsp
Shallots	6, peeled
Onion	1, peeled and cubed
Garlic	3 cloves, peeled
Young ginger	2-cm knob, peeled

Method

▌ Season fish with 1/2 tsp salt and pepper. Set aside.

▌ Heat oil in a pot. Lightly brown garlic and ginger. Add ground ingredients and cook until fragrant.

▌ Pour in tamarind juice and bring to the boil.

▌ Add remaining salt and sugar, polygonum leaves and fish. Reserve some leaves for garnishing if desired.

▌ Cook until done and serve.

indian fish curry with bitter gourd

Ingredients

Black pomfret (*ikan bawal hitam*)	1, medium-sized, cut whole fish into slices	Tamarind pulp (*asam Jawa*)	2 Tbsp, mixed with 4 Tbsp water and strained
Salt	1 tsp	Coconut cream	250 ml, squeezed from 1 grated coconut with sufficient water added
Cooking oil	4 Tbsp		
Garlic	5 cloves, peeled and sliced		
Onions	2, peeled and sliced	Coconut milk	750 ml, squeezed from same grated coconut with sufficient water added
Curry leaves	3 sprigs, stems discarded		
Fenugreek seeds (*halba*)	1 tsp		
Ginger	2.5-cm knob, peeled and ground	Bitter gourd	1, seeds and membranes scraped off, cut into 4-cm wide pieces and soaked in salted water
Turmeric (*kunyit*)	2.5-cm, peeled and ground		
Fish curry powder	2 rounded (heaped) Tbsp, mixed with 65 ml water	Salt	1 tsp or to taste
		Sugar	1 tsp or to taste

Method

1 Season fish with 1 tsp salt. Set aside for 15 minutes.

1 Heat oil in a wok. Brown garlic and onions. Add curry leaves and fenugreek, as well as ground ginger and turmeric. Fry for a few minutes.

1 Add curry powder paste and fry until fragrant. Add tamarind juice and coconut milk, then bring to the boil.

1 Add drained bitter gourd pieces and simmer for 5 minutes, then add fish. Simmer until fish is cooked and bitter gourd tender.

1 Pour in coconut cream, then adjust to taste with salt and sugar. Serve.

indian fish head curry

Ingredients

Red snapper *(ikan merah)* fish head	1, about 1.3 kg, either kept whole or chopped into large pieces	Coconut milk	625 ml, squeezed from same grated coconut with sufficient water added
Salt	1 tsp		
Cooking oil	2 Tbsp	Aubergine (eggplant/brinjal)	1, roll cut
Onion	1, peeled and sliced		
Fish curry powder	2 Tbsp, mixed with 4 Tbsp water to form a paste	Salt	2 tsp or to taste
		Curry leaves	5 sprigs, stems discarded
Mustard seeds	1 tsp		

Ingredients to be ground (processed)

Tamarind pulp *(asam Jawa)*	2 tsp, mixed with 125 ml water and strained
Coconut cream	250 ml, squeezed from 1 grated coconut with sufficient water added

Dried chilli paste	1 Tbsp
Fresh red chillies	10, seeded
Shallots	120 g, peeled
Lemon grass *(serai)*	2 stalks

Method

▌ Season fish head with 1 tsp salt. Set aside for at least 15 minutes.

▌ Heat oil in a pot and stir-fry onion for 1–2 minutes. Add ground ingredients and cook until fragrant.

▌ Add curry powder paste and mustard seeds. Cook for 1–2 minutes, then pour in tamarind juice and coconut milk. Bring to the boil.

▌ Add aubergine pieces and adjust to taste with remaining salt. When aubergine pieces are half-cooked, add curry leaves, coconut cream and then fish head. Cook for 5–6 minutes.

▌ Serve hot with rice.

Note: To roll cut, first lay the vegetable on its side. Starting at the stem end, make a 45° cut, then roll vegetable 180° either towards or away from you and cut at the same angle. Repeat, alternating rolling directions, until vegetable is completely cut up.

laksa johor

Ingredients

Dried anchovy (ikan bilis) stock	3.5 litres
Fish curry powder	10 level Tbsp
Lemon grass (serai)	1 stalk, bruised
Polygonum leaves (daun kesum)	12 sprigs, stems discarded
Torch ginger buds (bunga kantan)	2, split
Dried sour fruit (asam gelugur)	3 pieces
Grated coconut	3 Tbsp, pan-fried without oil until golden brown and ground
Spanish mackerel (ikan tenggiri)	6 slices, steamed and flaked
Coconut cream	500 ml, squeezed from 2¹/₂ grated coconuts with sufficient water added
Salt	3 tsp or to taste
Fresh thick round rice (laksa) noodles	1.5 kg, scalded, or rice vermicelli (bee hoon)

Ingredients to be ground (processed) (A)

Shallots	15, peeled
Onions	2, peeled
Garlic	6 cloves, peeled
Galangal (lengkuas)	2.5-cm knob, peeled
Ginger	3-cm knob, peeled
Lemon grass (serai)	2 stalks, sliced
Dried prawn (shrimp) paste (belacan)	5 x 5 x 1-cm piece

Ingredients to be ground (processed) (B)

Dried prawns (shrimps)	3 Tbsp, rinsed
Fried anchovies (ikan bilis)	100 g

Complementary ingredients

Long (snake) beans	10–12, cut into 2.5-cm lengths and boiled
Onions	3, peeled and finely sliced
Cucumber	1, shredded
Torch ginger bud (bunga kantan)	1, sliced
Bean sprouts	300 g, scalded
Kalamansi limes (limau kesturi)	8–10, halved
Preserved radish (chai poh)	2 Tbsp, chopped

Method

1 In a large pot, combine anchovy stock, curry powder, lemon grass, polygonum leaves, torch ginger buds and dried sour fruit slices. Bring to the boil.

1 Add ground ingredients (A), followed by grated coconut, then ground ingredients (B). Simmer over low heat for 30 minutes.

1 Add flaked fish, coconut cream and salt to taste.

1 To serve, divide rice noodles into serving bowls and top with desired amounts of complementary ingredients. Ladle hot soup over.

nyonya fish head curry with bunga kantan

Ingredients

Fish head	1, large, halved, use mangrove snapper *(ikan jenahak)*, red snapper *(ikan merah)* or Spanish mackerel *(ikan tenggiri)*
Salt	1 tsp
Ground white pepper	1/2 tsp
Torch ginger buds *(bunga kantan)*	2
Cooking oil	3 Tbsp
Onions	2, medium-sized, peeled and ground
Aubergine (eggplant/brinjal)	1, roll cut (see pg 56)
Water	625 ml
Tamarind pulp *(asam Jawa)*	60 g, mixed with 125 ml water and strained

Salt	1 1/2 tsp or to taste
Sugar	1 rounded (heaped) tsp or to taste
Tomatoes	2, quartered

Ingredients to be ground (processed)

Dried chillies	12, soaked and seeded
Fresh red chillies	5
Lemon grass *(serai)*	2 stalks
Galangal *(lengkuas)*	2.5-cm knob, peeled
Turmeric *(kunyit)*	2.5-cm knob, peeled
Dried prawn (shrimp) paste *(belacan)*	2.5 x 5 x 1-cm piece

Method

▌ Season fish head with 1 tsp salt and pepper. Set aside.

▌ Separate outer petals and stems of torch ginger buds and reserve them whole. Finely slice inner buds and set aside.

▌ Heat oil in a deep saucepan. Fry ground ingredients and onions over low heat until fragrant.

▌ Throw in whole parts of torch ginger buds. Stir-fry for 2–3 minutes.

▌ Add aubergine pieces and toss well. Pour in water and tamarind juice, then add salt and sugar to taste.

▌ When liquid reaches the boil, add fish head and return to the boil.

▌ Reduce heat and add tomatoes and torch ginger bud slices. Simmer for 6–7 minutes more or until fish is cooked and aubergine pieces are tender.

salted fish, snake gourd and spinach curry

Ingredients

Cooking oil	1 Tbsp
Galangal (*lengkuas*)	3-cm knob, peeled and smashed
Salam leaves (*daun salam*)	3–4
Sugar	1½ tsp
Salt	½ tsp
Water	600 ml
Low-fat milk	400 ml
Salted threadfin (*ikan kurau/senangin*)	90 g, rinsed, thinly sliced and pre-fried
Young corn	2 ears, each cut into 4 pieces
Snake gourd (*ketola ular*)	350 g, cut into 1.5–2-cm cubes
Spinach	200 g
Pure coconut cream (*pati santan*) (optional)	1 Tbsp
Salt	to taste

Ingredients to be ground (processed)

Shallots	7, peeled
Garlic	3 cloves, peeled
Red chillies	5, seeded
Candlenuts (*buah keras*)	5
Ground white pepper	1 rounded (heaped) tsp
Dried prawn (shrimp) paste (*belacan*) granules	1 tsp, pan-fried without oil
Turmeric (*kunyit*)	2-cm knob, peeled

Method

❙ Heat oil in a pot. Fry ground ingredients over low heat until fragrant, about 2 minutes.

❙ Add galangal and *salam* leaves. Continue to cook over low heat for 8 minutes.

❙ Stir in sugar, salt, water and low-fat milk. Bring to the boil.

❙ Add fried salted fish, corn and snake gourd. Simmer for 5–6 minutes.

❙ Add spinach and continue to cook until snake gourd is soft.

❙ Stir in coconut cream, if used, and adjust to taste with salt before serving.

Note: To toast dried prawn paste for storing, chop a block of it into small pieces and pan-fry them without oil until grainy and fragrant. Leave granules to cool before transferring to a jar with a tight-fitting lid and store in the refrigerator. The granules are now ready for use whenever you need it.

prawn and cincaluk in perut ikan mixture

Ingredients

Cooking oil	4 Tbsp
Preserved shrimps (cincaluk)	2 Tbsp
Prawns (shrimps)	300 g, medium-sized, peeled and cleaned
Preserved fish stomach (perut ikan)	300 g, washed in several changes of water and cut into 1-cm wide pieces
Long (snake) beans	200 g, cut into 2-cm lengths
French beans	200 g, cut into 2-cm lengths
Pineapple	350 g, peeled, cored and cut into wedges
Torch ginger buds (bunga kantan)	2, finely sliced
Pineapple pulp	80 g, blended (processed) with 250 ml water until fine
Coconut milk	600 ml, squeezed from 1 grated coconut with sufficient water added
Tamarind pulp (asam Jawa)	50 g, mixed with 625 ml water and strained
Salt	2 tsp or to taste

Ingredients to be ground (processed)

Dried chillies	30, cut into smaller pieces and soaked
Lemon grass (serai)	3 stalks, sliced
Shallots	10, peeled
Torch ginger buds (bunga kantan)	4, outer petals only
Galangal (lengkuas)	1-cm knob, peeled
Dried prawn (shrimp) paste (belacan)	1-cm cube piece
Turmeric (kunyit)	1-cm knob, peeled, or 1 tsp ground turmeric

Ingredients to be finely sliced (combined)

Kaffir lime leaves (daun limau purut)	25
Polygonum leaves (daun kesum)	10 sprigs, stems discarded
Pointed pepper leaves (daun kaduk)	100 leaves
Mint leaves	10 sprigs

Method

I Heat oil in a deep saucepan. Fry ground ingredients over medium heat for 5 minutes.

I Add preserved shrimps, prawns and preserved fish stomach pieces. Fry until half-cooked.

I Add long beans, French beans and pineapple pieces. Toss to cook vegetables, then add torch ginger buds and blended pineapple pulp. Bring to the boil.

I Add coconut milk and simmer for 5 minutes before adding tamarind juice and salt to taste.

I Meanwhile, put sliced leaves into a colander and rinse under a running tap. Drain well. Allow to drip dry.

I Add washed leaves to simmering curry little by little. When done, return to the boil, then remove from heat. Serve with cooked rice or rice vermicelli (bee hoon).

Note: The curry tastes much better 2 hours after cooking. Also, be mindful to wash the leaves well under running water. This is to remove traces of the green sap that can make the curry look dull.

penang perut ikan

Ingredients

Preserved fish stomach (perut ikan)	450–500 g
Torch ginger buds (bunga kantan)	4
Cooking oil	2–3 Tbsp
Dried anchovies (ikan bilis)	50 g, rinsed and ground
Tamarind pulp (asam Jawa)	40 g, combined with 1.25 litres water and strained
Pointed pepper leaves (daun kaduk)	200 g, finely sliced
Turmeric leaves (daun kunyit)	6, finely sliced
Kaffir lime leaves (daun limau purut)	5, finely sliced
Carrot	1, roll cut into small pieces (see pg 56)
Aubergines (eggplants/brinjals)	2, small, roll cut into small pieces (see pg 56)
Long (snake) beans	200 g, cut into 2-cm lengths
Peeled pineapples	500 g, cut into 2-cm wide wedges
Sugar	2 Tbsp or to taste

Ingredients to be ground (processed)

Large onions	300 g, peeled and diced
Lemon grass (serai)	3 stalks, sliced
Garlic	2 cloves
Ginger	2-cm knob, peeled
Galangal (lengkuas)	3-cm knob, peeled
Red chillies	20, seeded
Bird's eye chillies (cili padi)	10
Dried prawn (shrimp) paste (belacan) granules	1 Tbsp
Ground black pepper	1 tsp
Ground white pepper	1/2 tsp

Method

❙ Wash preserved fish stomach in several changes of water. Drain and cut into 1-cm wide pieces.

❙ Seperate and reserve outer petals of torch ginger buds. Finely slice inner buds and set aside.

❙ Heat oil in a pot. Fry ground ingredients with outer petals of torch ginger bud until fragrant. Add dried anchovies and cook over low heat for 5 minutes.

❙ Add preserved fish stomach, then tamarind juice. Bring to the boil.

❙ Stir in all sliced leaves and simmer for about 20 minutes.

❙ Except sugar, add all remaining ingredients. Simmer for 40–50 minutes or until fish stomach is soft and gravy thick.

❙ Adjust to taste with sugar before serving.

curry fish head a la malaysia

Ingredients

Fish head	1, about 600 g, use threadfin (ikan kurau/ senangin), grouper (ikan kerapu) or red snapper (ikan merah)
Salt	1 tsp
Cooking oil	4 Tbsp
Tamarind pulp (asam Jawa)	20 g, mixed with 250 ml water and strained
Pure coconut cream (pati santan)	125 ml, squeezed from 1 grated coconut
Coconut milk	250 ml, squeezed from same grated coconut with sufficient water added
Lady's fingers (okra)	10
Onions	2, peeled and cut into rings
Tomatoes	2, halved
Salt	1 tsp or to taste
Torch ginger bud (bunga kantan)	1, finely sliced

Ingredients to be ground (processed)

Dried chillies	15, cut into smaller pieces and soaked
Fresh red chillies	5
Shallots	20, peeled
Garlic	5 cloves, peeled
Turmeric (kunyit)	3-cm knob, peeled and sliced
Galangal (lengkuas)	3 slices, peeled
Ground fennel (jintan manis)	1 Tbsp
Dried prawn (shrimp) paste (belacan) granules	1 rounded (heaped) tsp

Method

1. Halve fish head and season with 1 tsp salt. Set aside.

2. Heat oil in a 1.4 litre heatproof (flameproof) baking (casserole) dish. Fry ground ingredients over medium-low heat until fragrant.

3. Add tamarind juice and coconut milk. Bring to the boil.

4. Add lady's fingers, onions and tomatoes. When lady's fingers are cooked, add fish head and cook for 5–6 minutes.

5. Pour in coconut cream and stir in salt to taste. Turn off heat and sprinkle in torch ginger bud. Serve.

Note: To obtain coconut cream from grated coconut, place small portions of 1 grated coconut onto a piece of muslin cloth and squeeze. Do this several times until 125 ml of pure, coconut cream (pati santan) is obtained. Then, add 250 ml water to once-squeezed grated coconut and squeeze to obtain a thinner coconut milk.

65

curried

sardine and brinjal curry

Ingredients

Cooking oil	3 Tbsp		
Onion	1, peeled and sliced	Coconut milk	500 ml, squeezed from ½ grated coconut with sufficient water added
Garlic	2 cloves, peeled and sliced		
Ginger	2.5-cm, peeled and shredded	Tomatoes	2, quartered
Mustard seeds	1 tsp	Canned sardines *(ikan lemuru)* in tomato sauce	1 can (425 g)
Curry leaves	2 sprigs	Salt	1½ tsp
Fish curry powder	2 Tbsp, mixed with 2 Tbsp water to form a paste	Red chilli	1, sliced
		Green chilli	1, sliced
Aubergine (eggplant/brinjal)	1 brinjal, roll cut into small pieces (see pg 56)	Lime *(limau nipis)* or lemon juice	1 Tbsp

Method

▌ Heat oil in a wok. Fry onion slices until transparent. Add garlic, ginger, mustard seeds and curry leaves. Stir-fry until fragrant.

▌ Add curry paste and stir-fry over low heat for 2 minutes, then add aubergine pieces and stir-fry for 2 minutes more.

▌ Pour in coconut milk and simmer until aubergine pieces are soft.

▌ Add tomatoes and sardines together with tomato sauce. Either toss carefully to mix ingredients or break up whole sardines into small pieces with a wooden spoon.

▌ When liquid reaches the boil, reduce heat and simmer for 5 minutes.

▌ Add salt, then red and green chillies. Lastly, stir in lime or lemon juice.

▌ Serve with flat breads such as *roti canai*, *puri* or chapati.

south indian fish curry

Ingredients

Spanish mackerel (ikan tenggiri)	600 g, cut into steaks		
Salt	1 tsp		
Ground white pepper	1/4 tsp	Fish curry powder	3 Tbsp
Cooking oil	2 Tbsp	Tamarind pulp (asam Jawa)	1/2 Tbsp, mixed with 125 ml water and strained
Mustard seeds	1 tsp		
Fenugreek seeds (halba)	1/2 tsp	Coconut cream	125 ml, squeezed from 1/2 grated coconut with sufficient water added
Onions	2, peeled and sliced		
Shallots	5, peeled and sliced		
Garlic	2 cloves, peeled and sliced	Coconut milk	500 ml, squeezed from same grated coconut with sufficient water added
Fresh ginger	2 slices, peeled and finely shredded		
Green chillies	2, split	Tomatoes	2, quartered
Curry leaves	2 sprigs, stems discarded	Salt	to taste

Method

I Season fish with 1 tsp salt and pepper.

I Heat oil in a large saucepan. Fry mustard seeds until they pop, then add fenugreek seeds and fry until fragrant.

I Add onions, shallots, garlic and ginger. Stir-fry for 1–2 minutes.

I Add green chillies and curry leaves, then combined fish curry powder and tamarind juice.

I When liquid reaches the boil, add coconut milk and return to the boil.

I Add fish and tomatoes. Simmer for 5 minutes or until fish is just cooked.

I Pour in coconut cream and return to the boil. Remove from heat and add salt to taste.

I Serve hot.

Note: For variation, prepare this dish with black pomfret (ikan bawal hitam), barracuda (ikan alu-alu) or narrow-barred Spanish mackerel (ikan tenggiri batang).

stingray curry with pineapple

Ingredients

Stringray (ikan pari)	800 g, cut into bite-sized pieces
Salt	1 1/2 tsp
Ground black pepper	1/2 tsp
Ground white pepper	1/2 tsp
Cooking oil	3 Tbsp
Onion	1, large, peeled and cut into 8 wedges
Fresh pineapple	400 g, peeled and cut into wedges
Coconut cream	250 ml, squeezed from 1 grated coconut with sufficient water added
Coconut milk	500 ml, squeezed from same grated coconut with sufficient water added
Fish sauce	2 Tbsp
Sugar	1 1/2 tsp
Salt	to taste
Thai sweet basil leaves	20 g

Ingredients to be ground (processed)

Red chillies	12, seeded
Lemon grass (serai)	3, sliced
Young galangal (lengkuas)	2-cm knob, peeled
Coriander leaves (cilantro)	6 short sprigs, snipped with scissors or chopped
Kaffir lime leaves (daun limau purut)	2, central stems discarded
Freshly ground black pepper	1 tsp
Dried prawn (shrimp) paste (belacan) granules	1 rounded (heaped) tsp
Ground turmeric (kunyit serbuk)	2 rounded (heaped) tsp
Ground cumin (jintan putih serbuk)	2 rounded (heaped) tsp

Method

I Season fish with salt and peppers and set aside.

I Heat oil in a deep saucepan. Fry onion wedges until transparent.

I Add ground ingredients and fry over medium heat for 8–10 minutes or until fragrant.

I Stir in pineapple pieces and pour in coconut milk. Bring to the boil.

I Stir in fish sauce, sugar and salt to taste.

I When liquid reaches the boil, add fish and cook for 3 minutes.

I Pour in coconut cream and stir in basil, then return to the boil.

I Reduce heat and simmer for 3 minutes or until fish is cooked through. Serve.

penang fish curry

Ingredients

Spanish mackerel (ikan tenggiri)	about 600 g, sliced
Salt	I tsp
Cooking oil	2 Tbsp
Fish curry powder	2 Tbsp, mixed with a little water to form paste
Torch ginger bud (bunga kantan)	I, sliced
Curry leaves	3 sprigs
Coconut milk	500 ml, squeezed from $^{1}/_{2}$ grated coconut with sufficient water added
Salt	to taste
Lady's fingers (okra)	8, steamed
Tomatoes	3, quartered

Ingredients to be ground (processed)

Shallots	6, peeled
Garlic	3 cloves, peeled
Ginger	2.5-cm knob, peeled
Lemon grass (serai)	I stalk, sliced

Method

I Season fish I tsp salt and set aside.

I Heat oil in a pot. Fry ground ingredients over low heat until fragrant.

I Add curry powder paste and fry for a few seconds, then add torch ginger bud and curry leaves. Cook until fragrant.

I Pour in coconut milk and bring to the boil. Add fish and simmer for 5 minutes.

I Stir in salt to taste. Add lady's fingers and tomatoes. Simmer until fish is cooked.

I Serve hot.

fish and sweet potato curry

Ingredients

Fish fillet	350 g, use threadfin (*ikan kurau/senangin*), grouper (*ikan kerapu*) or golden snapper (*ikan ungar*)
Salt	1 tsp
Ground white pepper	1/2 tsp
Butter	1 Tbsp
Cooking oil	4 Tbsp
Sweet potatoes	500 g, peeled and cut into 2.5-cm cubes
Cooking oil	2 Tbsp
Onion	1, peeled and finely chopped
Garlic	4 cloves, peeled and finely chopped
Chopped coriander leaves (cilantro)	2 Tbsp
Water	250 ml
Salt	1 tsp
Pure coconut cream (*pati santan*)	2 Tbsp

Ingredients to be ground (processed)

Dried chillies	4, pre-soaked and seeded
Dried prawn (shrimp) paste (*belacan*)	2.5-cm square piece
Galangal (*lengkuas*)	2.5-cm knob, peeled
Lemon zest	2 tsp
Lemon grass (*serai*)	1 stalk, sliced
Water	125 ml

Spices (combined)

Ground coriander (*ketumbar serbuk*)	1 Tbsp
Ground cumin (*jintan putih serbuk*)	2 tsp
Ground turmeric (*kunyit serbuk*)	1 tsp
Paprika	2 tsp

Method

- Season fish with salt and pepper and set aside.
- Heat butter and 4 Tbsp oil in a wok. Fry sweet potatoes over low heat until cooked through, about 15 minutes. Drain and set aside.
- Heat 2 Tbsp oil in a clean wok, add onion and garlic and fry until fragrant.
- Add ground ingredients and fry for 5 minutes.
- Add combined spices and chopped coriander. Cook for 2 minutes, then add water and salt.
- Return sweet potatoes and add fish to wok. Bring to the boil.
- Stir in coconut cream and simmer for 2–3 minutes. Serve.

deep- &
shallow-fried

deep-fried fish with black pepper

Ingredients

Fish fillet	300 g, cut into 1-cm thick slices, use grouper (ikan kerapu) or red snapper (ikan merah)	Sesame oil	1/2 tsp
		Egg white	1, beaten with a fork
Salt	1 tsp	Cooking oil for deep-frying	
Ground white pepper	1/2 tsp	Potato or tapioca flour	3 Tbsp
Crushed black peppercorns	1 tsp	Chilli sauce of choice	to taste

Method

❚ Season fish slices with salt, peppers and sesame oil. Set aside for 15 minutes, then stir in beaten egg white.

❚ Heat sufficient oil for deep-frying.

❚ Coat fish slices thoroughly with potato or tapioca flour, then deep-fry until crisp and light golden.

❚ Serve with chilli sauce.

clay pot fish head

Ingredients

Fish head	1, about 800 g, use grouper (ikan kerapu), threadfin (ikan kurau/ senangin) or red snapper (ikan merah)	Onion	1, peeled and cut into 6 wedges
		Dried Chinese mushrooms	4, soaked to soften and stems discarded
Chinese rice wine	1/2 Tbsp		
Light soy sauce	1/2 Tbsp	Canned button mushrooms	6–8
Ginger juice	1/2 Tbsp	Red chillies	2, sliced
Ground white pepper	1/2 tsp	Spring onions (scallions)	2, cut into 2.5-cm lengths
Cooking oil for deep-frying		Corn flour (cornstarch)	1/2 Tbsp, mixed with 1 Tbsp water to make thickener
Soft bean curd	1 square, cut into 2.5-cm cubes		
Cooking oil	3 Tbsp	Lettuce or salad leaves of choice	6–8, washed
Ginger	2.5-cm knob, peeled		

Batter (combined)

Egg	1, beaten
Corn flour (cornstarch)	2 rounded (heaped) Tbsp
Water	2 Tbsp

Sauce (combined)

Chicken stock	250 ml
Oyster sauce	$1/2$ Tbsp
Light soy sauce	$1/2$ Tbsp
Chinese rice wine	2 tsp
Sesame oil	1 tsp
Sugar	1 tsp
Ground white pepper	$1/2$ tsp

Method

▌ Clean fish head thoroughly. Season with wine, soy sauce, ginger juice and pepper. Leave for 30 minutes.

▌ Heat sufficient oil for deep-frying in a wok. Coat fish head with batter, then deep-fry each side for 5–8 minutes or until golden brown and cooked. Drain and set aside.

▌ Lower bean curd cubes into hot oil and deep-fry for 2 minutes. Drain and set aside.

▌ Heat 3 Tbsp oil in a clay pot. Sauté ginger and onion until fragrant. Add Chinese mushrooms and stir-fry for 1 minute.

▌ Add button mushrooms and chillies and toss briskly. Pour in combined sauce ingredients and bring to the boil.

▌ Add fried fish head and bean curd pieces. Reduce heat a little, cover and simmer for 5–8 minutes.

▌ Add spring onions and thickener. Remove from heat when gravy is thickened.

▌ Arrange lettuce or salad leaves along sides of clay pot and serve immediately. Sufficient for 4 people with 2 other dishes.

Note: For Muslims, the Chinese rice wine in this recipe can be omitted without seriously affecting the overall taste of the dish. Also, the lettuce or salad leaves in this recipe are mainly for garnishing. For lettuce, the Chinese (sang choy), butterhead or cos (romaine) varieties are suitable.

fillet of fish with tom yam sauce

Ingredients

Fish fillets	500 g, cut into 5-cm thick slices, use golden snapper *(ikan ungar)* or red snapper *(ikan merah)*		
Cooking oil for deep-frying		*Tom yam* paste	30 g
Egg	1, small, beaten with a fork	Fresh chicken stock or water	60 ml
Corn flour (cornstarch)	50 g	Sugar	2 tsp
Cooking oil	2 Tbsp	Mayonnaise	100 ml
Lemon grass *(serai)*	2 stalks, hard outer layers discarded and finely sliced	Spring onions (scallions)	2, cut into 2-cm pieces
Torch ginger bud *(bunga kantan)*	1, outer petals discarded and inner bud finely sliced	**Seasoning**	
		Salt	1 tsp
Red chilli	1, seeded and finely sliced	Light soy sauce	1 tsp
Bird's eye chillies *(cili padi)*	10, finely sliced	Sugar	1/2 tsp
		Ground white pepper	1/4 tsp

Method

❚ Season fish pieces with seasoning ingredients. Set aside for 15 minutes.

❚ Heat sufficient oil for deep-frying. Coat fish well with egg, then corn flour before deep-frying for 2–3 minutes or until crisp, golden and cooked through. Drain well and arrange on serving plate.

❚ Heat 2 Tbsp oil in a clean saucepan. Stir-fry lemon grass, torch ginger bud and chilli slices.

❚ Stir in *tom yam* paste and pour in chicken stock or water. Bring to the boil.

❚ Stir in sugar, then remove from heat. Stir in mayonnaise.

❚ Pour gravy over fish. Garnish with spring onions and serve.

deep-fried fish with black beans

Ingredients

Firm fish fillet	500 g, cut into 2.5-cm cubes, use grouper (ikan kerapu), threadfin (ikan kurau/senangin) or red snapper (ikan merah)
Cooking oil for deep-frying	
Cooking oil	1 Tbsp
Garlic	3 cloves, peeled and crushed
Fermented black beans (tau see)	1 Tbsp or 20 g, chopped
Red chillies	1–2, seeded and chopped
Chinese rice wine	½ Tbsp
Spring onion (scallion)	1, diagonally sliced into 1-cm wide pieces

Seasoning

Salt	1 tsp
Ground white pepper	½ tsp
Egg white	1, lightly beaten
Corn flour (cornstarch)	2 tsp

Sauce (combined)

Fresh chicken stock or water	125 ml
Sugar	1 tsp
Light soy sauce	3 tsp
Sesame oil	½ tsp
Corn flour (cornstarch)	2 tsp

Method

▎ Season fish cubes with seasoning ingredients. Leave for at least 15 minutes.

▎ Heat sufficient oil for deep-frying in a wok. Deep-fry fish for 1 minute, then drain well.

▎ Heat 1 Tbsp oil in a clean wok. Lightly brown garlic, then add black beans and chillies. Cook for 15 seconds.

▎ Splash in wine, then pour in combined sauce ingredients.

▎ When liquid reaches the boil and thickens, add fish and spring onion pieces; reserve some for garnishing if desired. Toss gently until well mixed.

▎ Garnish as desired and serve hot with rice.

Note: For Muslims, the Chinese rice wine in this recipe can be omitted without seriously affecting the overall taste of the dish.

fried or steamed fish topped with bunga kantan sambal

Ingredients

Whole fish	400 g, cleaned, use queen fish *(ikan talang)*, sole *(ikan lidah/sebelah)*, sea bass *(ikan siakap)* or trout *(ikan trout)*
Salt	1 tsp
Ground white pepper	1/4 tsp
Cooking oil	2 Tbsp
Torch ginger buds *(bunga kantan)*	2, outer petals separated and reserved, inner buds finely sliced
Tamarind pulp *(asam Jawa)*	2 tsp, mixed with 190 ml water and strained
Sugar	2–3 tsp
Kaffir lime leaves *(daun limau purut)*	2–3, shredded
Lime *(limau nipis)* juice	extracted from 1 large lime
Lemon grass *(serai)* for garnishing	

Ingredients to be ground (processed)

Dried chillies	8
Red chillies	5
Shallots	10, peeled
Garlic	3 cloves, peeled
Lemon grass *(serai)*	1 stalk, sliced
Dried prawn (shrimp) paste *(belacan)*	2.5-cm cube piece

Method

▌Season fish with salt and pepper. Set aside for 30 minutes.

▌Meanwhile, prepare *sambal* (chilli paste). Heat oil in a wok. Fry ground ingredients with outer petals of torch ginger buds until fragrant.

▌Add tamarind juice and sugar. Bring to a slow boil.

▌Stir in torch ginger bud slices and lime leaves. Lastly, stir in lime juice. Remove from heat.

▌Deep-fry or steam fish for 10 minutes, then pour *sambal* over cooked fish.

▌Garnish as desired with lemon grass and serve hot.

deep-fried fish with fruity sauce

This is a healthy dish; tender fried fish steaks with a crunchy, fruity and sweet-and-sour-tasting sauce.

Ingredients

Fish steaks	3, use threadfin (ikan kurau/senangin), grouper (ikan kerapu) or red snapper (ikan merah)	Potato flour for coating	
		Cooking oil	1 Tbsp
Salt	1 tsp	Onion	1, peeled and cut into 1.5-cm cubes
Ground white pepper	1 tsp		
Potato flour	1/2 Tbsp, combined with 2 Tbsp water	Canned or fresh pineapple	2 slices, diced
		Green apple	1/2, peeled, cored and diced
Egg	1, beaten with a fork		
Cooking oil for deep-frying		Red chillies	2, seeded and diced
		Fruity sauce*	250 ml, see recipe below

Method

I Rub fish with salt, pepper and potato flour paste. Add beaten egg and mix. Set aside for 30 minutes.

I Heat sufficient oil for deep-frying in a wok or saucepan. Coat fish well with potato flour, then deep-fry until light golden. Drain and place on absorbent kitchen paper.

I Heat 1 Tbsp oil in a clean wok. Lightly sauté onion, pineapple, apple and chillies. Pour in fruity sauce.

I Return fish to wok and carefully mix well. Dish out onto a serving dish and serve hot.

*Fruity sauce

Tomato sauce (ketchup)	1 small bottle (325 ml)		
Chilli sauce	1 small bottle (325 ml)		
Pineapple jam	1 jar (450 g), preferably of Season's brand	Cider vinegar	3 Tbsp
		Lemon juice	1 Tbsp
Mixed fruit jam	1 jar (450 g), preferably of Season's brand	Salt	1 1/2 tsp
		Sesame oil	1 tsp

Method

I In a deep non-stick saucepan, combine tomato and chilli sauces, jams and vinegar. Cook over medium heat, stirring with a wooden spoon, until jams completely dissolve.

I When mixture reaches the boil and thickens, stir in lemon juice, salt and sesame oil. Remove from heat.

I Allow to cool, then store in a clean, covered jar. The sauce will keep for 4–5 weeks refrigerated and longer frozen.

dry fried fish head

Ingredients

Fish head	800 g-1 kg, chopped into 3 x 5-cm pieces, use grouper *(ikan kerapu)* or red snapper *(ikan merah)*
Cooking oil for deep-frying	
Cooking oil	1 Tbsp
Chopped garlic	1 Tbsp
Chopped shallots	1 Tbsp
Chopped ginger	1/2 Tbsp
Red chilli	1, seeded and chopped
Chinese cooking wine *(hua tiao)*	1 Tbsp
Spring onions (scallions)	2, chopped

Seasoning

Salt	1 tsp
Sugar	1 tsp

Sesame oil	1 tsp
Ground white pepper	1/2 tsp
Ginger juice	1 Tbsp
Light soy sauce	1 Tbsp
Chinese cooking wine *(hua tiao)*	1 Tbsp
Corn flour (cornstarch)	1 Tbsp

Sauce (combined)

Chilli bean sauce	2 Tbsp
Plum sauce	2 Tbsp
Light soy sauce	1 Tbsp
Salt	1/2 tsp
Sugar	1/2 tsp
Fresh chicken stock	150 ml

Method

1. Season fish head with seasoning ingredients. Leave for 1 hour.

2. Heat sufficient oil for deep-frying. Cook fish head for 6–8 minutes or until brown. Drain well.

3. Heat 1 Tbsp oil in a clean wok. Lightly brown garlic, shallots, ginger and chilli. Pour in combined sauce ingredients.

4. When liquid reaches the boil, return fish head to wok. Stir gently to coat fish head with sauce, taking care not to break flesh into pieces.

5. Drizzle in wine and carefully toss well. Dish out and top with spring onions to serve.

Note: For Muslims, the Chinese cooking wine in this recipe can be omitted without seriously affecting the overall taste of the dish.

sliced fish in black bean sauce mix

Ingredients

Any firm white fish fillet	250–300 g, cut into 1.5 x 4-cm slices		
Cooking oil for deep-frying		Shallot	1, peeled and sliced
Egg white	1, beaten	Red chillies	2, cut into strips
Corn flour (cornstarch) for coating		Black bean sauce mix	1 sachet (50 g), mixed with 150 ml water
Cooking oil	1 Tbsp	Spring onions (scallions)	1–2, cut into 2.5-cm lengths
Young celery	1 stalk, sliced	Sesame oil	1 tsp
Carrots	90 g, peeled if desired, sliced and parboiled		
Cooking oil	1 Tbsp	**Seasoning (combined)**	
Ginger	4 slices, peeled and shredded	Salt	1/4 tsp
		Sugar	1/4 tsp
		Sesame oil	1 tsp
Garlic	2 cloves, peeled and minced	Light soy sauce	2 tsp
		Chinese rice wine	2 tsp

Method

❚ Season fish slices with seasoning ingredients. Leave for 15–20 minutes.

❚ Heat sufficient oil for deep-frying. Meanwhile, add beaten egg white to fish slices and mix, then coat slices thickly with corn flour before deep-frying until light golden brown. Drain in a colander.

❚ Heat 1 Tbsp oil in a clean wok. Stir-fry celery and carrots for 1 minute. Remove and set aside.

❚ Heat 1 Tbsp oil in wok and lightly brown ginger, garlic and shallot. Add chillies, celery and carrots. Toss briskly before returning fish to wok.

❚ Add black bean sauce mix. Cook for 1 minute, then stir in spring onions and sesame oil. Dish out and serve.

Note: For Muslims, the Chinese rice wine in this recipe can be omitted without seriously affecting the overall taste of the dish.

fish nuggets with creamy wasabi dip

Ingredients

Fish fillet	350 g, cut into 3-cm cubes, use salmon *(ikan salmon)*, grouper *(ikan kerapu)* or red snapper *(ikan merah)*
Salt	¹/₂ tsp
Sugar	¹/₂ tsp
Ground white pepper	¹/₄ tsp
Cooking oil for deep-frying	

Batter

Plain (all-purpose) flour	75 g
Baking powder	¹/₂ tsp
Bicarbonate of (baking) soda	¹/₄ tsp
Salt	¹/₄ tsp
Water	125 ml
Sesame oil	¹/₂ tsp

Creamy Wasabi Dip (combined)

Mayonnaise	60 g
Salad cream	1 Tbsp
Prepared wasabi	1¹/₂ tsp

Method

1 Season fish cubes with salt, sugar and pepper. Leave for 15 minutes.

1 Combine dry batter ingredients in a bowl. Add water and stir to form a smooth batter, thick enough to coat back of spoon. Stir in sesame oil.

1 Heat sufficient oil for deep-frying. Dip each piece of fish into batter before lowering into hot oil. Cook for 1–2 minutes or until golden.

1 Serve fish nuggets with Creamy Wasabi Dip and your salad of choice.

fish with wasabi cream sauce

Ingredients

Fish fillet	500 g, cut into 2 x 4-cm pieces, use salmon (*ikan salmon*), grouper (*ikan kerapu*) or red snapper (*ikan merah*)
Salt	1 tsp
Light soy sauce	1 tsp
Sugar	1/2 tsp
Ground white pepper	1/4 tsp
Egg	1, small, beaten with a fork
Cooking oil for deep-frying	
Corn flour (cornstarch) or potato flour	60 g

Cooking oil	1 Tbsp
Lettuce of choice for garnishing	

Sauce (combined)

Mayonnaise	100 ml
Wasabi	4 tsp
Fresh chicken stock or water	75 ml
Salt	1/2 tsp

Method

▮ Season fish pieces with salt, soy sauce, sugar and pepper. Set aside for 15 minutes, then add beaten egg and mix well with fish pieces.

▮ Heat sufficient oil for deep-frying. Coat fish slices thoroughly with flour, then deep-fry until crisp and light golden. Drain and set aside.

▮ Heat 1 Tbsp oil in a clean wok. Add combined sauce ingredients and stir well.

▮ When liquid reaches the boil, turn off heat and add fish. Toss gently to coat fish with sauce, then dish out onto a bed of lettuce.

▮ Alternatively, arrange fried fish on a serving dish lined with lettuce leaves and spoon sauce over.

▮ Serve with rice.

deep- & shallow-fried

fried fish with pine nuts

Ingredients

Grouper (ikan kerapu) fillet	500–600 g, cut into 2 x 3-cm pieces	Chicken stock	3 Tbsp
Cooking oil for deep-frying		Corn flour (cornstarch)	1/2 Tbsp, mixed with 2 Tbsp water to make thickener
Pine nuts	100 g		
Cooking oil	1 Tbsp	Sesame oil	1 tsp
Ginger	4 slices, peeled and minced		
Garlic	3 cloves, peeled and sliced	**Seasoning (combined)**	
		Salt	1 tsp
Spring onion (scallion)	1, cut into 2.5-cm lengths	Ground white pepper	1/4 tsp
Carrot slices	14, parboiled	Egg white	1
Chinese cooking wine (hua tiao)	1 Tbsp	Corn flour (cornstarch)	1 Tbsp
Sugar	1/2 tsp	Cooking oil	1 Tbsp, to be mixed in last
Salt	1/2 tsp		

Method

▌ Season fish pieces with combined seasoning ingredients. Set aside.

▌ Heat sufficient oil for deep-frying, but not until too hot. Deep-fry pine nuts for 1–2 minutes. Drain and spread out on paper-lined tray to cool.

▌ Reheat oil until very hot, then deep-fry fish pieces. Drain and set aside.

▌ Heat 1 Tbsp oil in a clean wok. Add ginger, garlic and spring onion and stir-fry until fragrant, then add carrot slices and return fish to wok.

▌ Drizzle in wine and add sugar, salt and stock. Bring to a quick boil.

▌ Stir in thickener and drizzle in sesame oil. Add pine nuts, toss and serve.

Note: For Muslims, the Chinese cooking wine in this recipe can be omitted without seriously affecting the overall taste of the dish.

tuna fish balls

Ingredients

Mashed potatoes	360 g		
Canned tuna *(ikan tongkol)* in oil	1 can (185 g), drained		
Red chilli	1, seeded and minced	Dry sherry	2 Tbsp
Chopped parsley	1/2 Tbsp	Butter	20 g
Chopped spring onion (scallion)	1/2 Tbsp	Plain (all-purpose) flour	2 Tbsp, seasoned with a dash each of salt and ground white pepper
Shallots	2, peeled and finely chopped		
Ground white pepper	1/2 tsp	Egg	1, beaten
Salt	1 tsp	Fresh white breadcrumbs	100 g
Cajun seasoning	1 tsp	Cooking oil for deep-frying	
Dried oregano (optional)	1/2 tsp	Chilli sauce of choice	to taste

Method

❚ Mash potatoes and drained tuna together until well combined.

❚ Add chilli, parsley, spring onion, shallots, pepper, salt, cajun seasoning, oregano, sherry and butter. Mix well to blend.

❚ Portion and shape mixture into 20 walnut-sized balls.

❚ Roll balls lightly in flour, then in beaten egg before coating with breadcrumbs.

❚ Deep-fry crumbed balls in hot oil until golden.

❚ Serve with chilli sauce.

Note: For Muslims, the dry sherry in this recipe can be omitted without seriously affecting the overall taste of the dish.

fried kembung with sambal kicap

Ingredients

Chubb mackerels (ikan kembung) or whitings (ikan bulus-bulus/pasir-pasir)	5	Prepared mustard	1 tsp
		Light soy sauce	1 tsp
Cooking oil for deep-frying			

Sambal Kicap Dip (combined)

Dark soy sauce	1 Tbsp
Dried prawn (shrimp) paste (belacan) granules	1 Tbsp, roasted by dry-frying in a pan
Kalamansi lime (limau kesturi) juice	extracted from 2 limes, or 1 Tbsp lemon juice
Sugar	1 tsp

Seasoning

Salt	1/2 tsp
Ground white pepper	1/4 tsp
Ground turmeric (kunyit serbuk)	1/2 tsp

Method

❙ Season fish with seasoning ingredients. Set aside for 30 minutes.

❙ Combine dip ingredients in a small bowl. Mix well and set aside.

❙ Heat sufficient oil for deep-frying until hot. Deep-fry fish until cooked through, then drain.

❙ Serve with Sambal Kicap Dip.

kedgeree fish cakes with tomato salsa

Ingredients

Any firm, white-fleshed fish fillet	450 g		
Salt	a dash	Chopped parsley	1 1/2 Tbsp
Ground white pepper	a dash	Chopped coriander leaves (cilantro)	1 1/2 Tbsp
Saffron threads	1/2 tsp, or 2 tsp curry powder for a spicy flavour	Green chillies	3, seeded and finely chopped
Salt	1 tsp	Ground white pepper	1/2 tsp
Rice	180 g, washed	Salt	to taste
Butter	30 g	Egg	1, beaten
Dhal	100 g, soaked in water for 4 hours	Dried breadcrumbs	120 g
Salt	1/2 tsp	Cooking oil for deep-frying	
Hard-boiled eggs	2, shelled and finely chopped	Salsa sauce*	1 recipe, see opposite

Method

▌ Steam fish fillet until cooked. When done, drain fish and reserve stock. Skin and finely flake fish meat. Season fish flakes with a dash each of salt and pepper. Set aside.

▌ Add saffron threads and 1 tsp salt to washed rice. Cook rice with reserved fish stock, adding more water if necessary. When cooked rice is fluffy and soft, stir in butter. Chicken stock can be used in place of fish stock.

▌ Meanwhile, cook dhal in sufficient water with $^1/_2$ tsp salt until soft. Transfer softened dhal to an electric blender (processor) and blend until fine.

▌ Combine fish flakes, rice, dhal, hard-boiled eggs, parsley, coriander, green chillies and $^1/_2$ tsp pepper. Adjust to taste with more salt if desired.

▌ Portion and shape combined ingredients into 14 fish cakes. Dip each fish cake into beaten egg and coat with breadcrumbs.

▌ Heat sufficient oil for deep-frying. Cook fish cakes on both sides until golden and crisp. Drain on paper towels.

▌ Serve with Salsa sauce.

*Salsa sauce

Tomatoes	2, large, peeled and chopped		
Grated or finely chopped onion	1 Tbsp	Salt	$^1/_2$ tsp or to taste
Green capsicum (bell pepper)	$^1/_2$, small, finely chopped	Ground black pepper	$^1/_4$ tsp
Garlic	2 cloves, peeled and crushed	Lemon juice	extracted from $^1/_2$ a small lemon, or 1 Tbsp red pesto basil sauce
Green chilli	1, seeded and finely chopped	Fresh chopped parsley	1 Tbsp
Ground cumin (jintan putih serbuk)	$^1/_2$ tsp	Chopped coriander leaves (cilantro)	1 Tbsp

Method

▌ Combine all ingredients and mix well.

▌ Place in refrigerator and leave to macerate until required.

fried lemon fish

Ingredients

Fish fillet	600 g, cut into 2 x 3-cm pieces, use golden snapper *(ikan ungar)*, red snapper *(ikan merah)*, salmon *(ikan salmon)*, or grouper *(ikan kerapu)*
Cooking oil for deep-frying	
Corn flour (cornstarch)	2 Tbsp
Cooking oil	I Tbsp

Seasoning

Light soy sauce	I Tbsp
Sesame oil	I tsp
Salt	1/2 tsp
Ground white pepper	1/4 tsp

Sauce (combined)

Plum sauce	3 Tbsp
Water	2 Tbsp
Lemon juice	3 Tbsp
Sugar	2 Tbsp

Garnishing (optional)

Butterhead, baby cos (romaine) or Chinese *(sang choy)* lettuce leaves	
Coriander leaves (cilantro)	

Method

I Season fish pieces with seasoning ingredients. Set aside for 15 minutes.

I Heat sufficient oil for deep-frying. Coat fish pieces with corn flour, then deep-fry for 2 minutes or until golden. Drain and set aside.

I Heat 1 Tbsp oil in a clean wok. Pour in combined sauce ingredients.

I When liquid reaches the boil and thickens, add fish pieces and toss gently until coated with sauce.

I Serve hot on a bed of lettuce and topped with coriander leaves if desired.

fried battered whitings with indonesian sambal

Ingredients

Whitings (ikan bulus-bulus/pasir-pasir)	15–16, cleaned and heads removed
Salt	1 tsp
Ground white pepper	1/2 tsp
Cooking oil for deep-frying	

Batter

Self-raising flour	55 g
Rice flour	30 g
Baking powder	1 tsp
Salt	1/2 tsp
Water	120 ml
Kalamansi lime (limau kesturi) juice	2 tsp
Holy basil for garnishing	

Sambal (chilli paste)

Cooking oil	1 Tbsp
Shallots	3, peeled and coarsely pounded
Garlic	1 clove, peeled and minced
Red chillies	3, coarsely pounded
Dried prawn (shrimp) paste (belacan) granules	1 rounded (heaped) tsp
Tomato	1/2, medium, chopped
Sugar	1/2 tsp
Salt	1/2 tsp
Water	2 Tbsp

Method

▌ Season fish with salt and pepper and set aside.

▌ Prepare batter. Sift flours and baking powder into a mixing bowl. Stir in salt. Separately combine water and lime juice, then pour over dry ingredients. With a fork, mix well until a smooth batter results. Set aside for 30 minutes.

▌ Meanwhile, prepare sambal. Heat oil in a saucepan. Fry shallots for a few seconds, then add garlic and fry until fragrant. Add chillies and mix well, cooking for 1 minute. Stir in all remaining ingredients. Cook until tomato pieces are softened and sambal is dry.

▌ Heat an electric deep-fryer to 175°C. Dip fish in batter, then fry for 5 minutes or until golden brown. Drain on absorbent paper towels.

▌ Garnish and serve fried fish with sambal.

nyonya fried fish with spicy plum sauce

Ingredients

Whole fish	500 g, use tilapia or African fish *(ikan tilapia)*, grouper *(ikan kerapu)*, threadfin *(ikan kurau/ senangin)* or sea bass *(ikan siakap)*
Salt	1 tsp
Ground white pepper	1/4 tsp
Cooking oil for deep-frying	
Cooking oil	2 Tbsp
Shallots	8, peeled and finely sliced
Garlic	4 cloves, peeled and finely sliced
Young ginger	2.5-cm knob, peeled and chopped
Red chillies	2, seeded and chopped
Torch ginger bud *(bunga kantan)*	1, outer petals discarded and inner bud finely sliced
Kaffir lime leaves *(daun limau purut)*	3, 2 finely sliced and 1 shredded
Crisp-fried shallots	2 Tbsp
Spring onions (scallions)	2, chopped

Sauce (combined)

Fresh chicken or dried anchovy *(ikan bilis)* stock	125 ml
Plum sauce	3 Tbsp
Tomato sauce (ketchup)	3 Tbsp
Chilli sauce	2 Tbsp
Lime *(limau nipis)* juice	1 Tbsp
Sesame oil	1 tsp
Sugar	2 Tbsp
Ground white pepper	1/2 tsp
Salt	1 tsp

Method

I Make 2 diagonal slits on each side of fish. Season with salt and pepper and set aside.

I Heat sufficient oil for deep-frying in a wok. Fry fish on both sides until lightly browned and cooked through. Drain and place onto a serving dish.

I Heat 2 Tbsp oil in a clean wok. Fry shallots, garlic, ginger and chopped chillies until fragrant.

I Stir in torch ginger bud and kaffir lime leaf slices, then pour in combined sauce ingredients. Bring to the boil.

I Pour sauce mixture over fish on serving dish. Garnish with crisp-fried shallots, chopped spring onions and shredded kaffir lime leaf.

I Serve.

fish with spicy black vinegar sauce

Ingredients

Sea bream (ikan kerisi)	500 g, or any whole freshwater fish	Corn flour (cornstarch)	2 tsp, mixed with 2 Tbsp chicken stock or water to make thickener
Salt	I tsp		
Ground white pepper	1/2 tsp		
Cooking oil for deep-frying		**Sauce (combined)**	
Corn flour (cornstarch) for coating		Clear chicken stock	150 ml
		Light soy sauce	3/4 Tbsp
Cooking oil	2 Tbsp	Sugar	45 g
Garlic	2 large cloves, peeled	Black rice vinegar	30 ml
Fresh ginger	2.5-cm knob, peeled and minced	Salt	I pinch
Red chilli	I, seeded and minced	**Garnishing**	
Spring onions (scallions)	2, chopped	Coriander leaves (cilantro)	
		Chilli strips (optional)	

Method

I Score fish deeply. With a sharp knife at a 30° angle, diagonally score one side of fish starting 4 cm from gill opening. Lightly score a criss-cross on tail end. Repeat on the other side. If cuts are deep enough, sections of flesh will part from the central bone to become flaps by virtue of their weight.

I Season fish with salt and pepper. Leave for 15–20 minutes.

I Heat sufficient oil for deep-frying in a wok. Coat fish well with corn flour, ensuring surfaces exposed after scoring are also well coated.

I Lower fish into hot oil holding its tail and with splayed belly side down. As soon as fish is immersed, use a pair of pincers or tongs to pull fish out by the tail.

I Hold fish upside down for 2 minutes or until flesh flaps set. Return fish to hot oil and deep-fry until batter is crisp and golden brown, takes 4–5 minutes. Remove and place on a warmed serving dish.

I Heat 2 Tbsp oil in a clean wok. Add garlic and ginger and stir-fry for 30 seconds or until fragrant. Add chilli and combined sauce ingredients. Stir and bring to a rapid boil.

I Add spring onions. Re-stir thickener and gradually stir into boiling sauce. Remove and pour over fish.

I Garnish as desired and serve immediately.

fried tom yam fish

Ingredients

Firm fish fillet	300 g, cut into 2 x 4-cm pieces, use grouper *(ikan kerapu)*, red snapper *(ikan merah)* or salmon *(ikan salmon)*
Tom yam paste	I Tbsp
Chilli paste	I Tbsp
Fish sauce	2 tsp
Rice flour	2–3 Tbsp
Cooking oil for deep-frying	

Lemon grass *(serai)*	2 stalks, sliced
Kaffir lime leaves *(daun limau purut)*	5
Basil leaves *(daun selasih)*	10

Ingredients to be ground (processed)

Onion	I, peeled
Garlic	4–5 cloves, peeled
Ginger	10-cm knob, peeled

Garnishing

Cucumber slices

Tomato slices

Method

❚ Put fish pieces in a large mixing bowl.

❚ In an electric blender (processor), combine ingredients to be ground and blend until fine. Strain to obtain juice.

❚ Transfer 2 Tbsp juice to a small mixing bowl. Add *tom yam* and chilli pastes and fish sauce. Mix well.

❚ Pour *tom yam* mixture over fish and mix well. Leave to marinate for at least 6 hours.

❚ Heat an electric deep-fryer to 175°C. Add rice flour to fish pieces and stir to mix, then deep-fry for 3 minutes or until cooked through and crispy.

❚ Garnish and serve.

vietnamese deep-fried fish cakes

Ingredients

Spanish mackerel (*ikan tenggiri*)	275 g, steamed and flaked		
Sweet potatoes	225 g, peeled, boiled and mashed	Egg	1, large, lightly beaten
		Rice flour for coating	
Ground white pepper	1/2 tsp	Cooking oil for deep-frying	
Pure coconut cream (*pati santan*)	2 Tbsp		
Tomatoes	2, peeled and chopped	**Garnishing**	
Chopped coriander leaves (cilantro)	2 Tbsp	Shredded Chinese (*sang choy*) or iceberg lettuce leaves	
Fish sauce	1 Tbsp		
Light soy sauce	1 Tbsp	Sprigs of mint	

Method

1 Combine all ingredients in a large bowl.

1 Using a medium-sized ice-cream scoop, portion and shape mixture into round balls.

1 Roll balls in rice flour to coat.

1 Deep-fry floured balls in hot oil until golden brown and cooked through.

1 Serve garnished with lettuce and mint.

special sweet and sour fish

Although the sauce is what makes this a favourite dish for most people, the use of fresh, succulent fish adds a richness to the taste that makes it even more appetising.

Ingredients

Whole fish	750–900 g, cleaned, use red snapper (ikan merah), grouper (ikan kerapu), threadfin (ikan kurau/ senangin) or sea bass (ikan siakap)
Egg	less than 1/2, small, beaten with a fork
Cooking oil for deep-frying	
Potato flour for coating	
Chinese block or soft brown sugar	75 g, finely chopped
Potato flour	1 tsp, mixed with 1 Tbsp water to make thickener

Seasoning

Chicken stock granules	1 tsp
Salt	1/4 tsp
Ground white pepper	1/4 tsp

Potato flour	1 tsp, mixed with 1 Tbsp water

Vegetables (combined)

Onion	1, small-medium-sized, peeled and cut into 6 wedges
Red capsicum (bell pepper)	1/2, cut into 2-cm squares
Yellow or green capsicum (bell pepper)	1/2, cut into 2-cm squares
Fresh pineapple	1/2–1 slice, cut into triangles

Sauce (combined)

Brown sugar	75 g
Tomato sauce (ketchup)	1 rounded (heaped) Tbsp
A1 steak sauce	1 Tbsp
Salt	1/2 tsp
Cider vinegar	100 ml

Method

▌ Make 2 diagonal slits on each side of fish. Season with seasoning ingredients, then add beaten egg. Set aside for 30 minutes.

▌ Bring a small saucepan of water to the boil. Scald all vegetables for a few seconds. Drain and set aside.

▌ Heat sufficient oil for deep-frying. Coat fish with potato flour and deep-fry until light golden. Drain and set aside.

▌ In a non-stick pan, melt brown sugar over low heat. Stir in combined sauce ingredients and cook, stirring all the time, until sugar is dissolved.

▌ Add scalded vegetables and fried fish to sauce, then thickener.

▌ When gravy is thickened, dish out and serve hot.

thai fish cakes

This recipe makes approximately 30 pieces.

Ingredients

Spanish mackerel *(ikan tenggiri)*	1.2 kg
Water	100 ml, mixed with ½ tsp salt
Chilli paste*	3 Tbsp, about 145 g, see recipe
Pure coconut cream *(pati santan)*	2 Tbsp
Basil leaves *(daun selasih)*	5 sprigs, about 15 g, chopped
Cooking oil for deep-frying	
Chilli sauce of choice	to taste

*Chilli paste

Dried chillies	20, cut into small pieces, seeded, soaked and drained
Lemon grass *(serai)*	2 stalks, sliced
Young galangal *(lengkuas)*	3-cm knob, peeled and sliced
Kaffir lime peel *(kulit limau purut)*	3–4 slices
Kaffir lime leaves *(daun limau purut)*	3, sliced
Shallots	6, peeled
Garlic	10 cloves, peeled
Fresh red chillies	2, seeded
Dried prawn (shrimp) paste *(belacan)*	2.5 x 2.5 x 1-cm piece
Salt	2 tsp

Method

▌ Fillet fish and scrape meat from skin with a spoon. About 675 g of fish should result. Refrigerate while preparing chilli paste.

▌ In an electric food chopper, blend (process) all chilli paste ingredients without adding water until fine. Measure up 145 g of chilli paste to use in this recipe and set aside. Remaining paste can be frozen for future use.

▌ Using the same food chopper, blend ⅓ fish flesh with ⅓ salted water, then add ⅓ chilli paste and ⅓ coconut cream and blend again. Repeat process with remaining two-thirds of ingredients. Lastly, add basil leaves and blend for a few seconds.

▌ Using a medium-sized ice-cream scoop, portion and shape mixture into balls. Place on greased plates. Grease hands and lightly flatten balls into patties.

▌ In a large, shallow saucepan, heat sufficient oil for deep-frying. Fry patties in batches, each for 6–7 minutes or until golden brown.

▌ Serve with chilli sauce.

spicy butter red tilapia

Ingredients

Red tilapia or African fish (ikan tilapia)	350–400 g, head discarded	Curry leaves	3 sprigs, stems discarded
Salt	1 tsp	Red chillies	2, seeded and finely chopped
Ground white pepper	$^1/_2$ tsp	Bird's eye chillies (cili padi)	10, seeded and finely chopped
Tapioca flour	15 g		
Cooking oil for deep-frying		Sugar	1 rounded (heaped) tsp
		Salt	$^1/_2$ tsp
Butter	70 g	Nestum cereal	6 Tbsp, about 40 g

Method

1. Split fish into two halves horizontally, keeping the central bone on one half. Cut each half into 2.5-cm pieces.

2. Season fish pieces with 1 tsp salt and pepper. Set aside for 15 minutes.

3. Heat sufficient oil for deep-frying in a wok or electric deep-fryer (190°C). Just before deep-frying, coat fish pieces well with tapioca flour.

4. Lower flour-coated fish into hot oil and cook for 4–5 minutes or until crisp and golden. Drain and place onto absorbent kitchen paper.

5. Heat butter in a clean wok. Stir-fry curry leaves until fragrant, then add chillies, sugar and salt. Toss to mix well.

6. Add Nestum cereal and stir-fry until well combined. Return fish to wok and toss well before dishing out. Serve.

Note: This dish is as finger-licking good as the popular Butter Prawns. The crisp-fried fish takes on a light, flaky texture that is given an added lift by the aromatic combination of Nestum and curry leaves clinging to it. Although the inclusion of bones add flavour to the fish, deboned fillets can be used if the task of handling bones is preferably avoided.

terubuk with thai chilli sauce dip

Ingredients

Hilsa (ikan terubuk)	1 kg, cleaned but not scaled
Salt	1 tsp
Ground white pepper	1 tsp
Cooking oil for shallow-frying	
Coriander leaves (cilantro) for garnishing	

Light soy sauce	1 Tbsp
Shallots	6, peeled and sliced
Palm sugar (gula Melaka)	20 g
Red chilli	1, sliced
Bird's eye chillies (cili padi)	10, sliced
Coriander leaves (cilantro)	2 sprigs, chopped
Spring onion (scallion) (optional)	1, white part only, chopped

Thai Chilli Sauce Dip (combined)

Lemon juice	3 Tbsp
Fish sauce	1 Tbsp

Method

▌ Rub fish inside and out with salt and pepper. Set aside for 15 minutes.

▌ Heat sufficient oil in a wok to immerse half the fish.

▌ Lower in fish, cover wok and fry over medium heat for 10–12 minutes on each side or until cooked through. Drain.

▌ Garnish and serve fried fish with Thai Chilli Sauce Dip.

Note: This wonderful oily fish has lots of fine bones and you need time and patience to enjoy and savour the fish for its delightful aroma. Leaving the scales on when frying the fish keeps the flesh moist and tender. It is also popular when baked or grilled and served with sambal belacan (chilli paste dip).

stuffed sambal fish

Ingredients

Horse mackerel *(ikan cupak/bentong)*	4–6, medium-sized, slit along both sides of back bone
Salt	1 tsp
Tamarind pulp *(asam Jawa)*	1 tsp, mixed with 2 Tbsp water and strained
Kaffir lime leaves *(daun limau purut)*	2, finely sliced
Cooking oil for shallow-frying	

Ingredients to be ground (processed)

Shallots	6–8, peeled
Garlic	3 cloves, peeled
Dried prawn (shrimp) paste *(belacan)*	2.5 x 2.5 x 1-cm piece
Lemon grass *(serai)*	2 stalks
Dried chillies	5–6, seeded and soaked
Fresh chillies	4, seeded
Turmeric *(kunyit)*	5-cm knob, peeled
Salt	1/2 tsp
Cooking oil	2 Tbsp

Method

▌ Rub fish with salt and set aside.

▌ Place all to-be-ground ingredients into a blender (processor). Add 2 Tbsp water or more if required and blend until fine.

▌ Combine ground ingredients and tamarind juice in a saucepan. Over low heat, stir for 8–10 minutes or until fragrant.

▌ Stir in lime leaves, then remove from heat and allow *sambal* (chilli paste) to cool. Stuff fish, including stomach cavity, with *sambal*.

▌ Heat sufficient oil for shallow-frying in a wok. Lower in fish and cover wok. Fry fish on both sides until just cooked through.

grilled

fish steaks with spicy tangy plum sauce

This is a quick-to-prepare grilled dish that results in moist and juicy fish steaks with a piquant sauce enhanced by shallots and chillies. Bottled Thai chilli sauce is a sweet and tangy Thai-styled chilli dip made from sugar, chillies, garlic and salt.

Ingredients

Fish steaks	2, use grouper *(ikan kerapu)* or red snapper *(ikan merah)*
Salt	1 tsp
Ground white pepper	$^1/_2$ tsp
Cooking oil	1 Tbsp, for brushing
Cooking oil	2 Tbsp
Shallots	3, peeled and sliced
Garlic	3 cloves, peeled and chopped
Bird's eye chillies *(cili padi)*	10, chopped

Sauce (combined)

Thick plum sauce	2 Tbsp
Thai chilli sauce	2 Tbsp
Lemon juice	$2^1/_2$ Tbsp
Water	3 Tbsp
Chilli sauce	2 tsp
Sugar	1 tsp
Salt	$^1/_2$ tsp

Garnishing

Cooked crab roe
Crisp-fried shallots
Sprig of parsley

Method

▌ Season fish steaks with salt and pepper. Set aside for 15 minutes.

▌ Heat an electric table or oven grill to 200°C. Brush with 1 Tbsp oil and grill fish for 8–10 minutes or until just cooked, turning over halfway through cooking time. Transfer cooked steaks to a serving dish.

▌ Meanwhile, heat 2 Tbsp oil in a small saucepan. Lightly brown shallots and garlic. Add chillies and pour in combined sauce ingredients.

▌ When liquid reaches the boil and is slightly thickened, pour over fish steaks.

▌ Garnish as desired and serve.

grilled mayonnaise fish

Ingredients

Fish steaks	2–3, each 2-cm thick, use threadfin (ikan kurau/ senangin), grouper (ikan kerapu) or salmon (ikan salmon)	Thousand Island dressing	I Tbsp
		Chopped parsley	I tsp
Potatoes	3, about 240 g, peeled and cut into small cubes	Chopped spring onion (scallion)	I tsp
Ground white pepper	1/4 tsp	**Seasoning**	
Salt	1/4 tsp	Salt	I tsp
Chopped ham	50 g, or dry-fried chopped bacon	Ground white pepper	1/2 tsp
Margarine, butter or oil	I tsp	Tabasco sauce	2 tsp
Leek	6-cm length, white part only, finely diced	Dried dill	1/2 tsp
		Finely chopped parsley	I rounded (heaped) tsp
Fresh or canned button mushrooms	3, chopped	Finely chopped spring onion (scallion)	I rounded (heaped) tsp
Mayonnaise	2 Tbsp		

Method

❚ Mix fish pieces with seasoning ingredients. Leave for 30 minutes.

❚ Boil potato cubes for 10 minutes or until soft. Drain, mash and season with pepper and salt. Stir in chopped ham or bacon. Set aside.

❚ Heat margarine, butter or oil in a pan. Fry leek and mushrooms for I minute.

❚ Add to mashed potatoes, then stir in remaining ingredients.

❚ In a turbo broiler, grill fish pieces at 190°C for about 10 minutes. Turn over and grill for 1–2 minutes more.

❚ Spread potato mixture onto fish pieces. Grill for about 10 minutes or until brown.

grilled five-spice norwegian salmon

Grilling greatly heightens the aroma of salmon. The unique combination of a spicy, sweet and sour-tasting marinade makes this dish delicious and great for entertaining.

Ingredients

Norwegian salmon (*ikan salmon*) steaks	3, each about 2.5-cm thick		
Fresh parsley for garnishing		Light soy sauce	2 Tbsp
		Honey	3 Tbsp
Seasoning		Freshly ground black pepper	
Garlic	2 cloves, peeled and finely ground	Shallot oil	$1/2$ Tbsp
Young ginger	2.5 cm, peeled and finely ground	Fresh coriander leaves (cilantro) or dill	3 sprigs, chopped
Lemon juice	125 ml	Chopped fresh parsley	1 Tbsp
Five-spice powder	$1/4$ tsp		

Method

I In a shallow heatproof (flameproof) dish, combine all seasoning ingredients. Add salmon steaks and leave to marinade for at least 3–4 hours.

I Grill marinated steaks in a turbo broiler or oven grill at 200°C for 12 minutes, turning over halfway through cooking time.

I Serve garnished with fresh parsley.

grilled fish drumsticks

Ingredients

Spanish mackerel (ikan tenggiri) meat	250 g, scraped from bones with a spoon
Peeled prawns (shrimps)	100 g
Sugar	1 Tbsp
Egg white	1
Seeded red chillies	3, 1 coarsely chopped and 2 cut into 5-cm strips
Cooking oil for greasing	
Lemon grass (serai)	9 stalks, each about 15–16 cm in length
Banana leaf	1

Ingredients to be ground (processed)

Shallots	5, peeled
Garlic	3 cloves, peeled
Salt	$1\frac{1}{4}$ tsp
Ground white pepper	$\frac{1}{2}$ tsp
Ginger	2-cm knob, peeled
Kaffir lime leaves (daun limau purut)	2
Cooking oil	1 Tbsp

Method

▌ When ingredients to be ground (processed) have been blended until fine, add fish meat, prawns and sugar. Blend for 1 minute or until well mixed.

▌ Add egg white and blend for 10–15 seconds more or until well combined.

▌ Transfer blended ingredients to a bowl. Stir in chopped chilli.

▌ Grease hands with a little oil. Take a stalk of lemon grass and wrap 1 Tbsp fish paste around thicker end to form a drumstick. Repeat until paste is used up.

▌ Decorate each drumstick with 2 chilli strips.

▌ Grease banana leaf with little oil. Place on oven rack or inside turbo broiler. Arrange drumsticks in 2 neat rows.

▌ Grill in oven or in turbo broiler at 190°C for 15 minutes.

▌ Garnish, if desired, with extra chilli strips and serve.

javanese grilled fish

Ingredients

Whole fish	1, about 600 g, use golden snapper *(ikan ungar)*, threadfin *(ikan kurau/senangin)* or red snapper *(ikan merah)*
Lime *(limau nipis)* juice	1 Tbsp
Salt	1 rounded (heaped) tsp
Cooking oil for deep-frying	

Seasoning (combined)

Ginger juice	1 Tbsp
Garlic	3 cloves, peeled and finely pounded
Salt	1 tsp

Sauce (combined)

Indonesian sweet soy sauce *(kecap manis)*	4 Tbsp
Cooking oil	1 Tbsp
Ground coriander *(ketumbar serbuk)*	1 Tbsp
Garlic	6 cloves, peeled and pounded
Sugar	1/2 tsp

Garnishing

Lettuce or salad leaves of choice
Cucumber slices
Lemon slices
Tomato wedges

Spicy Tomato Dip (combined)

Indonesian sweet soy sauce *(kecap manis)*	4 Tbsp
Shallot oil	1 Tbsp
Bird's eye chillies *(cili padi)*	6, sliced
Tomato	1, large, ripe, diced small
Shallots	4, peeled and sliced
Salt	a pinch

Method

I Rub fish with lime juice and salt inside and out. Leave for 15–20 minutes.

I Rinse fish under a running tap, drain and place onto an oval dish. Season with combined seasoning ingredients, then set aside for at least 1 hour.

I Heat sufficient oil for deep-frying in a wok. Cook fish until light golden brown, then drain.

I Preheat an electric table grill to 165°C. Place fish on top and brush with combined sauce ingredients. Grill for 5 minutes. Repeat with other side.

I Line serving dish with lettuce or preferred salad leaves. Place grilled fish on top. Garnish as desired with cucumber and lemon slices and tomato wedges.

I Serve with Spicy Tomato Dip.

salads, sambal
& pickles

nyonya nasi ulam

Ingredients

Rice	450 g (3 rice cups), washed and drained
Water	700 ml (4 rice cups)
Cooking oil for deep-frying	
Dried prawns (shrimps)	100 g, rinsed and coarsely chopped
Cooking oil	2–3 Tbsp
Salted threadfin (ikan kurau/senangin)	150 g, finely sliced
Ground white pepper	1 tsp
Shallots	12–15, sliced
Mint leaves for garnishing	

Ingredients to be finely shredded

Young ginger	5-cm knob, peeled
Young galangal (lengkuas)	5-cm knob, peeled
Pointed pepper leaves (daun kaduk)	40
Kaffir lime leaves (daun limau purut)	8
Turmeric leaves (daun kunyit)	3
Lesser galangal leaves (daun cekur)	8

Method

1 Cook rice with water in an electric rice cooker. When done, remove and leave to cool.

1 Meanwhile, heat sufficient oil for deep-frying in a wok. Cook dried prawns until fragrant and crispy, then drain and place in a blender (processor) and blend until fine. Set aside.

1 Reheat wok with 2–3 Tbsp oil. Fry salted fish until golden, then drain and leave to cool before blending in a mini blender (processor).

1 Combine dried prawns, salted fish, pepper, shallots and shredded ingredients. Add to rice and toss until all ingredients are well mixed.

1 Transfer rice to a serving dish and garnish. Serve cold.

sambal ikan bilis

Ingredients

Cooking oil	3 Tbsp
Tamarind pulp (asam Jawa)	2 tsp, mixed with 500 ml water and strained
Sugar	1 Tbsp
Salt	2 tsp or to taste
Anchovies (ikan bilis)	75 g, cleaned, oven-baked or pre-fried until crispy

Ingredients to be ground (processed)

Dried chillies	10, seeded and soaked
Fresh red chillies	6, seeded
Fresh turmeric (kunyit)	7-cm knob, peeled
Young ginger	2-cm knob, peeled
Shallots	16, peeled
Garlic	6 cloves, peeled
Dried prawn (shrimp) paste (belacan) granules	2 tsp

Method

❚ Heat oil and fry ground ingredients until fragrant. Stir in tamarind juice and bring to a slow boil.

❚ Stir in sugar and salt to taste, then add anchovies. Cook over medium-low heat until liquid is thick.

❚ Serve with coconut-flavoured rice (nasi lemak).

warm sesame norwegian salmon salad

Fresh Norwegian salmon has great appeal to gourmets. The smooth and firm flesh has an inviting colour and a delicate flavour. It makes a great ingredient for salads, combining well with an array of dressings. Try this for compliments.

Ingredients

Norwegian salmon (ikan salmon) fillet	400 g	Young ginger	1-cm knob, peeled and grated
Salt	1/2 tsp	Cider vinegar	2 Tbsp
Freshly ground black pepper	1/4 tsp	Light soy sauce	1 Tbsp
Lightly toasted sesame seeds	2 tsp	Sesame oil	1/2 Tbsp
Sunflower oil	3 Tbsp	Sugar	1/2 tsp
Garlic	3 cloves, peeled and crushed	Mixed salad leaves	120 g
		Cherry tomatoes	2–3, halved

Method

I Season salmon with salt, black pepper and sesame seeds. Firmly press sesame seeds down onto fish.

I Preheat an electric grill to 200°C. Grease tray with 1 Tbsp sunflower oil.

I Grill fish on both sides for 4–5 minutes or until golden brown and just cooked through.

I Meanwhile, heat remaining oil in a saucepan. Cook garlic and ginger for 1 minute, then add cider vinegar, soy sauce, sesame oil and sugar. Stir for a few seconds before removing from heat. Leave to cool to room temperature.

I Slice grilled salmon into desired serving portions and set aside. Toss mixed salad leaves in cooled dressing, then arrange on serving dish together with salmon pieces.

I Garnish with cherry tomatoes. Serve immediately.

nyonya acar fish

Ingredients

Mullets (ikan belanak)	1.5 kg, cleaned and heads discarded		
Salt	1 1/2 tsp		
Cooking oil for deep-frying		White vinegar	400 ml
Cooking oil	3 Tbsp	Water	250 ml
Peeled garlic	100 g, sliced	Sugar	375 g
Peeled old ginger	140 g, coarsely shredded	Salt	1 tsp
Salt	1/2 tsp	Green chillies	5, split and seeded
Cooking oil	2 Tbsp	Red chillies	5, split and seeded
Peeled fresh turmeric (kunyit)	60 g, sliced	Toasted sesame seeds	2 Tbsp

Method

▎ Season mullets with 1 1/2 tsp salt. Refrigerate for 10–15 minutes.

▎ Heat sufficient oil for deep-frying to 175°C. Pat dry mullets with paper towels, then deep-fry in hot oil until golden brown. Drain on absorbent kitchen paper.

▎ In a non-stick wok, heat 3 Tbsp oil and lightly brown garlic. Drain from oil and set aside.

▎ Reheat wok and lightly brown ginger with 1/2 tsp salt added. Dish out and set aside.

▎ Reheat wok with 2 Tbsp oil and stir-fry turmeric slices for 1 minute. Add vinegar and water, then bring to the boil.

▎ Add sugar and 1 tsp salt. Stir to dissolve sugar. When dissolved, reduce heat and simmer for 10 minutes or until liquid turns yellow.

▎ Remove syrup from heat and leave to cool thoroughly.

▎ Meanwhile, arrange mullets in a rectangular glass container with a cover, as do some baking (casserole) dishes. Scatter fried garlic and ginger, as well as chillies on top.

▎ Pour in sufficient cooled vinegar to completely immerse ingredients, then sprinkle on sesame seeds.

▎ Cover container and refrigerate at least overnight or for 1 day before serving.

norwegian salmon yee sang

Come Chinese New Year and it is time again to *lou hei* (stir up good fortune) with *yee sang* (raw fish). Most Chinese restaurants beckon with sumptuous *yee sang* meals, a dish that has stirred itself to sophisticated heights. It began with a simple combination of colourful vegetables, fruits, pickles and flour crisps with raw fish, mainly thin slivers of raw Chinese carp, and a tempting, tangy plum sauce. Nowadays, the ingredients include jellyfish, shark's fin, abalone and the ever popular salmon. Although you can find *yee sang* in almost all restaurants, you may like to try making your own. Here is a *yee sang* recipe using Norwegian salmon.

Ingredients

Norwegian salmon (ikan salmon)	120 g, thinly sliced	Preserved red ginger	25 g
Roasted peanuts (groundnuts)	40 g, coarsely ground	Pickled Chinese cucumber	25 g
Toasted sesame seeds	20 g	Pickled papaya	25 g
Coriander leaves (cilantro)	3–4 sprigs, chopped	Pickled leek	30 g, sliced
Flour crisps	200 g	Peeled Chinese pears	30 g
Red yam crisps	25 g	Red chilli	1, seeded
Green yam crisps	25 g	Kaffir lime leaves (daun limau purut)	2
Candied lime (kat paeng)	1/2		
Peanut (groundnut) oil	2 Tbsp		
Lime (limau nipis)	1, halved		

Spices

Five-spice powder	1/4 tsp
Ground cinnamon	1/4 tsp
Ground white pepper	1/4 tsp
Salt	1/4 tsp

Ingredients to be finely shredded

White (Chinese) radish	300 g, peeled
Carrots	200 g, peeled
Cucumber	100 g
Ginger	25 g, peeled

Sauce (combined)

Plum sauce	80 g
Orange marmalade	1 Tbsp
Warm water	1 Tbsp

Method

I Of the finely shredded ingredients, wrap radish shreds with a piece of white muslin cloth and squeeze out juices. Repeat with carrots. This will keep the vegetables dry.

I Except peanut oil and lime, arrange all other ingredients, including those finely shredded, on a large serving dish.

I Sprinkle on spices, then pour on combined sauce ingredients and peanut oil. Lastly, squeeze lime juice over the top and serve immediately.

steamed

easy otak-otak

Ingredients

Spanish mackerel (ikan tenggiri) fillet	300 g, thinly sliced
Salt	1/2 tsp
Ground white pepper	1/4 tsp
Pure coconut cream (pati santan)	150 ml
Eggs	3, large, lightly beaten with a fork
Aluminium foil patty cases	8, about 10 cm in diameter

Garnishing

Chinese lettuce (sang choy) leaves
Cucumber slices
Tomato slices

Paste

Dried chillies	8, soaked and seeded
Red chillies	5
Candlenuts (buah keras)	3
Young turmeric leaves (daun kunyit)	2, 10 cm in length, cut into pieces
Kaffir lime leaves (daun limau purut)	4
Galangal (lengkuas)	15 slices
Shallots	6, peeled
Turmeric (kunyit)	6-cm knob, peeled
Dried prawn (shrimp) paste (belacan) granules	1 tsp
Salt	2 tsp
Sugar	1 tsp

Method

1 Season fish with salt and pepper. Leave for 15 minutes.

1 Blend (process) all paste ingredients with sufficient coconut cream to form a fine paste. When done, transfer to a large bowl.

1 Add remaining coconut cream and beaten eggs to bowl and mix well. Add fish and stir to mix well again.

1 Fill patty cases with fish paste. Steam filled patty cases over rapidly boiling water for 15 minutes.

1 Garnish as desired and serve with rice.

Note: Pati santan is coconut cream derived from squeezing grated coconut without any added water.

otak-otak pulau pinang

Ingredients

Threadfin (ikan kurau/ senangin)	I kg, central portion
Salt	I tsp
Eggs	6
Salt	3 tsp
Kaffir lime leaves (daun limau purut)	32, finely sliced
Pure coconut cream (pati santan)	315 ml, squeezed from 1½ coconuts, grated
Banana leaves for wrapping	
Pointed pepper leaves (daun kaduk)	20
Bamboo skewers	

Ingredients to be ground (processed)

Dried chillies	10, soaked
Shallots	8, peeled
Garlic	3 cloves, peeled
Lemon grass (serai)	4 stalks
Galangal (lengkuas)	4 slices, peeled
Turmeric (kunyit)	2.5-cm knob, peeled
Dried prawn (shrimp) paste (belacan)	1.25-cm cube piece
Candlenuts (buah keras)	6
Ground coriander (ketumbar serbuk)	2 Tbsp
White peppercorns	36

Method

▌ Wash and halve fish, then cut each half into 5 × 4-cm pieces. Season with I tsp salt and leave for 15 minutes.

▌ Lightly beat eggs with a fork. Stir in ground ingredients, 3 tsp salt and sliced lime leaves. Mix with coconut cream.

▌ Soften banana leaves over heat, then cut into 15 × 18-cm rectangles. Make sure leaves have no holes or slits so ingredients will not seep through. Wash and dry softened leaves.

▌ At the centre of each prepared banana leaf, place a pepper leaf and a piece of fish. Fold as shown and fasten with a bamboo skewer. Trim top neatly with scissors.

▌ Steam parcels for 20 minutes or until cooked.

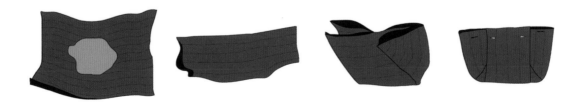

garlic steamed fish

Ingredients

White pomfret *(ikan bawal putih)* or Chinese pomfret *(ikan bawal tambak)*	1, 600–750 g, cleaned
Salt	1 tsp
Sugar	1/2 tsp
Ground white pepper	1/4 tsp
Cooking oil	2 Tbsp
Dried Chinese mushrooms	4–6, soaked, stems discarded and minced
Garlic	6–8 cloves, peeled and finely minced
Red chilli	1, seeded and finely minced
Spring onion (scallion)	1 stalk, chopped
Coriander leaves (cilantro)	2 sprigs, chopped
Rice vermicelli *(bee hoon)*	300 g, scalded

Sauce

Chicken stock	315 ml
Light soy sauce	2 1/2 Tbsp
Dark soy sauce	1/2 Tbsp
Sesame oil	1 tsp
Salt	1/4 tsp

Method

▌ Season fish with salt, sugar and pepper. Leave for 15–30 minutes.

▌ Combine all sauce ingredients in a bowl. Set aside.

▌ Heat oil in a skillet (frying pan). Stir-fry mushrooms for 1 minute or until fragrant.

▌ Add half the garlic and chilli; reserve some for garnishing if desired. Stir until golden brown, then dish into sauce ingredients. Stir in remaining raw garlic and pour sauce over fish.

▌ Steam fish over rapidly boiling water for 12–15 minutes or until cooked.

▌ Garnish with spring onion, coriander leaves and minced chilli if using.

▌ Serve with scalded rice vermicelli or steamed rice.

steamed fish, cantonese style

A healthy, classic steamed fish dish that brings out the wonderful flavour and texture of fresh fish. Subtly laced with soy sauce, each bite is tender and succulent.

Ingredients

Whole fish	1, 600-700 g, use Chinese pomfret *(ikan bawal tambak)*, grouper *(ikan kerapu)*, threadfin *(ikan kurau/senangin)* or sea bass *(ikan siakap)*
Young ginger	30 g, peeled and finely shredded
Red chilli	1/2, seeded and finely shredded
Spring onions (scallions)	2, cut into 5-cm lengths and shredded
Shallot or peanut (groundnut) oil	1 Tbsp
Sesame oil	1/2 Tbsp
Coriander leaves (cilantro)	2 sprigs

Seasoning

Coarse or plain salt	1 tsp
Sesame oil	1 tsp

Sauce (combined)

Light soy sauce	1 1/2 Tbsp
Dark soy sauce	1 tsp

Method

1. Make 2 diagonal slits on each side of cleaned fish. Dab fish dry with a paper towel and place on a heatproof (flameproof) plate.

2. Rub fish all over with seasoning ingredients and leave for 10–15 minutes.

3. Scatter ginger and red chilli shreds on top of fish, then steam over rapidly boiling water for 12 minutes.

4. Remove steamer cover. Scatter spring onion shreds on top of fish, then drizzle on combined sauce ingredients.

5. Combine both oils and heat until smoking hot, then pour over fish immediately.

6. Garnish with coriander leaves and serve hot with rice.

steamed fish in chilli soy bean paste

Ingredients

Whole fish	600 g, use horse mackerel *(ikan cupak/bentong)*, sea bream *(ikan kerisi)*, pony fish *(ikan kekek)* or mirror pomfret *(ikan cermin porong)*	Dried chillies	2, small, soaked, drained and chopped
Salt	¹/₂ tsp	Sweetened preserved soy bean paste *(taucu manis)*	I Tbsp
Sugar	¹/₂ tsp		
Ground white pepper	¹/₄ tsp	Chinese cooking wine *(hua tiao)*	I Tbsp
Sesame oil	I tsp	Light soy sauce	I tsp
Shallot or corn oil	I Tbsp	Fresh chicken stock (optional)	4 Tbsp
Garlic	2 cloves, peeled and minced	Spring onions (scallion)	2, cut diagonally into I-cm pieces
Ginger	5 slices, peeled and shredded		

Method

I Make 2 diagonal slits on each side of fish. Season with salt, sugar, pepper and sesame oil. Set aside.

I Heat shallot or corn oil in a small saucepan. Lightly brown garlic, ginger and dried chillies. Add soy bean paste and stir for I minute, then stir in wine and light soy sauce. Remove from heat.

I Allow stir-fried ingredients to cool, then spread on fish. If more gravy is preferred, drizzle chicken stock onto sides of fish.

I Steam fish over rapidly boiling water for 12–15 minutes.

I Garnish with spring onion bits and serve.

Note: For Muslims, the Chinese cooking wine in this recipe can be omitted without seriously affecting the overall taste of the dish. Also, if sweetened soy bean paste is unavailable, mix I tsp sugar with ¹/₂ Tbsp for a substitute.

steamed fish with spicy lemon plum sauce

The rich flavour of fresh fish is not lost when steamed and smothered with a delicious, spicy hot-sour sauce.

Ingredients

Grouper *(ikan kerapu)*	1, 600–700 g, cleaned
Salt	1 tsp
Ground white pepper	1/2 tsp
Cooking oil	2 Tbsp
Dried chillies	8, cut into 1-cm pieces, seeded and rinsed
Garlic	5 cloves, peeled and sliced

Sauce (combined)

Lemon juice	3 Tbsp
Plum sauce	2 Tbsp
Sugar	2 Tbsp
Fresh chicken stock	15 ml
Fish sauce	1 1/2 Tbsp

Toppings

Garlic	3 cloves, peeled and minced
Young ginger	3-cm knob, peeled and minced
Bird's eye chillies *(cili padi)*	10, chopped
Red chilli	1, chopped

Garnishing

Spring onions (scallions)	3, chopped
Coriander leaves (cilantro)	3 sprigs, chopped
Crisp-fried shallots (optional)	5–6 Tbsp

Method

❚ Season fish with salt and pepper. Place on a heatproof (flameproof) dish. Pour combined sauce ingredients over fish.

❚ Sprinkle topping ingredients over fish, starting with garlic and followed by ginger, bird's eye chillies and red chilli.

❚ Steam prepared fish over rapidly boiling water for 8 minutes.

❚ Meanwhile, heat oil in a saucepan. Add dried chillies and toss, then add garlic slices and toss for a few seconds more.

❚ Pour dried chilli and garlic mixture over cooked fish. Top with some spring onions, coriander leaves and crisp-fried shallots, if using.

❚ Spread remaining garnishing ingredients around fish and serve.

Note: The steamed grouper has a smooth, delicate texture that combines delightfully with a crunchy, subtly piquant sauce to give a fine balance of flavours.

2-style steamed and fried fish

Ingredients

Chinese pomfret (ikan bawal tambak)	1, about 1.2 kg	Fish sauce	1 Tbsp
Cooking oil	5 Tbsp	Sugar	2 tsp
Spring onion (scallion)	1, white part only	Dried anchovy (ikan bilis) granules	1 tsp
Ginger	1 thick slice, peeled	Chinese cooking wine (hua tiao)	2 tsp
Chinese cooking wine (hua tiao)	1 Tbsp	Dark soy sauce	1/4 tsp
Cooking oil	1 Tbsp		
Sesame oil	1 tsp	**Garnishing**	
Cooking oil	3 Tbsp	Spring onions (scallions)	2, cut into 6-cm lengths and finely shredded
Sauce		Coriander leaves (cilantro)	2–3 sprigs, cut into 6-cm sections and finely shredded
Fresh chicken stock	100 ml		
Oyster sauce	1 1/2 Tbsp		
Light soy sauce	1 1/2 Tbsp		

Method

▌ Use a sharp cleaver to slice one side of fish along the edges, separating 2.5 cm of flesh from the bones. Turn fish over and make fine slits across other side with cleaver at an angle.

▌ Heat 5 Tbsp oil in a shallow saucepan until very hot. Lower fish into oil slits side down. There should be enough oil to fry underside of fish.

▌ Place spring onion and ginger on top of fish. Cover saucepan, reduce heat and cook for 5 minutes.

▌ Reduce heat some more and allow fish to shallow-fry for 20 minutes more or until brown and crisp.

▌ Remove cover and test surface of fish with a skewer for doneness. Upper surface should have texture and appearance of steamed fish.

▌ When fish is cooked through, drain oil from saucepan. Then, drizzle in wine. Transfer fish to a serving dish, fried side up.

▌ Heat 1 Tbsp oil in a clean saucepan. Add sauce ingredients and bring to the boil. Drizzle in sesame oil. Carefully pour sauce onto underside of fish.

▌ Heat 3 Tbsp oil in a clean saucepan until hot and pour over fish. Garnish and serve hot.

Note: For Muslims, the Chinese cooking wine in this recipe can be omitted without seriously affecting the overall taste of the dish.

thai steamed fish

Ingredients

Whole fish	1, about 600 g, cleaned, use sea bass *(ikan siakap)* or red snapper *(ikan merah)*
Chopped spring onions (scallions) for garnishing	

Marinade

Red chillies	4, seeded and sliced
Bird's eye chillies *(cili padi)*	3–4, seeded and sliced
Lemon grass *(serai)*	3 stalks, sliced
Cooking oil	1 1/2 Tbsp
Torch ginger bud *(bunga kantan)*	1, medium, sliced
Kaffir lime leaves *(daun limau purut)*	3, finely sliced
Coriander (cilantro) roots	2, finely chopped
Fish sauce	1 Tbsp
Sugar	1/2 Tbsp

Method

▮ Prepare marinade. Blend (process) both chillies and lemon grass together until fine.

▮ Heat oil in a small saucepan and fry blended mixture over medium–low heat for 3–5 minutes or until fragrant. Remove from heat and leave to cool.

▮ To cooled mixture, add remaining marinade ingredients and mix well.

▮ Make 2 diagonal cuts on each side of fish, then rub marinade all over fish including inside slits and stomach.

▮ Steam fish over rapid boiling water for 12 minutes or until just cooked.

▮ Garnish and serve.

steamed fish with chinese pickled lettuce

Ingredients

Fish	600 g, cleaned, use *ampurau*, threadfin *(ikan kurau/senangin)*, red snapper *(ikan merah)* or sea bass *(ikan siakap)*	Young ginger	3-cm knob, peeled and finely shredded
Salt	I tsp	Garlic	2 cloves, peeled and finely minced
Ground white pepper	¹/₂ tsp	Red chilli	I, seeded and finely shredded
Pickled lettuce	I can (182 g)	Spring onions (scallions)	2, cut into 3-cm lengths
Chinese cooking wine *(hua tiao)*	I Tbsp	Coriander leaves (cilantro)	1–2 sprigs, cut into 3–4-cm lengths
Shallot oil	I Tbsp		

Method

▌ Season fish with salt and pepper. Leave for 15 minutes.

▌ Meanwhile, drain liquid from pickled lettuce can into a bowl. Store pickled lettuce in a covered container and refrigerate for future use.

▌ Combine pickled lettuce liquid and wine, then pour over fish. Drizzle shallot oil on top. Spread ginger, garlic and some red chilli over fish.

▌ Steam over rapidly boiling water for 12–15 minutes. To ensure that condensation collected under steamer cover does not drip onto fish, wrap cover with a tea towel.

▌ Top with remaining chilli, spring onions and coriander leaves. Serve.

Note: The ampurau is a freshwater fish found in Sarawak. It needs clean running water to thrive and can grow up to more than 10 kg in weight. The fish is not easy to obtain and can cost about RM300 per kg. The flesh of cooked ampurau is very fine, smooth, tender and sweet.

The reserved pickled lettuce can be sliced and eaten with porridge or minced together with chicken or pork and steamed. For Muslims, the Chinese cooking wine in this recipe can be omitted without seriously affecting the overall taste of the dish.

steamed fish with mapo doufu sauce

Ingredients

Whole fish	1, 600–700 g, cleaned, use parrot fish (ikan bayan), red snapper (ikan merah), threadfin (ikan kurau/ senangin) or grouper (ikan kerapu)
Salt	$1/2$ tsp
Ground white pepper	$1/2$ tsp
Shallot oil	1 tsp
Cooking oil	1 Tbsp
Chopped garlic	1 Tbsp
Chopped ginger	1 Tbsp
Preserved soy bean paste (tau cheo)	2 Tbsp (70 g), minced
Red chilli	1, seeded and minced
Minced chicken	75 g, seasoned with $1/4$ tsp salt and pepper

Fresh chicken stock	250 ml
Sesame oil	1 tsp
Soft bean curd	1 small piece (150 g), diced
Corn flour (cornstarch)	2 tsp, mixed with 1 Tbsp water to make thickener

Sauce

Light soy sauce	1 Tbsp
Rice wine	1 Tbsp
Black vinegar	$1^1/4$ Tbsp
Sugar	1 level Tbsp
Ground white pepper	$1/4$ tsp

Method

▌ Clean fish and drain well. Make 2–3 diagonal slits on each side of fish.

▌ Season fish with salt, pepper and shallot oil. Set aside for 15 minutes.

▌ Combine sauce ingredients and pour over fish, then steam over rapidly boiling water for 15 minutes.

▌ Heat cooking oil in a wok. Lightly brown garlic and ginger. Add soy bean paste and stir-fry for 1 minute.

▌ Add chilli and chicken and stir. When cooked, pour in stock and simmer for 1–2 minutes.

▌ Add sesame oil and bean curd, then thickener. Pour thickened sauce over fish and serve.

Note: For Muslims, the rice wine in this recipe can be omitted without seriously affecting the overall taste of the dish.

steamed fish with pickled plums & golden mushrooms

Ingredients

Whole fish	1, 600 g, cleaned, use golden pomfret *(ikan nyiur-nyiur)*, sea bass *(ikan siakap)*, red snapper *(ikan merah)*, grouper *(ikan kerapu)* or stingray *(ikan pari)*
Red chilli	1, seeded and minced
Garlic	4 cloves, peeled
Canned golden mushrooms	100 g
Cooking oil	2 Tbsp
Spring onions (scallions)	2, cut into 3-cm lengths

Seasoning

Salt	1 tsp
Sugar	1 tsp
Sesame oil	1 tsp
Corn flour (cornstarch)	1 tsp

Toppings

Pickled plums	2, pitted
Sugar	2 tsp
Garlic soy bean paste	2 Tbsp
Light soy sauce	1 Tbsp
Chinese rice wine	1 tsp

Method

I Make 2 diagonal slits on each side of fish. Rub seasoning ingredients all over fish. Transfer fish to a steaming plate.

I Combine topping ingredients and spread evenly over fish.

I Sprinkle half the chilli and garlic over topping layer. Distribute golden mushrooms along sides of fish.

I Steam fish over rapidly boiling water for 12 minutes.

I Meanwhile, heat oil in a wok. Stir-fry remaining chilli and garlic until golden. Dish out onto steamed fish. Sprinkle on spring onions and serve.

Note: For Muslims, the Chinese rice wine in this recipe can be omitted without seriously affecting the overall taste of the dish. Also, canned golden mushrooms can be replaced with fresh golden (enokitake) mushrooms. To use, trim off woody ends, rinse and pat dry with paper towels.

steamed siakap with thai asam sauce

Ingredients

Whole fish	1, about 1.5 kg, cleaned, use sea bass (ikan siakap), red snapper (ikan merah) or mirror pomfret (ikan cermin porong)		
Salt	1 tsp	Sugar	1/2 Tbsp
Ground white pepper	1/4 tsp	Salt	1 tsp
Shallot oil	1 Tbsp	Coconut	1/2, grated, mixed with 250 ml water, squeezed and strained
Torch ginger bud (bunga kantan)	2		
Cooking oil	3 Tbsp	**Ingredients to be ground (processed)**	
Onion	1, peeled and diced	Dried chillies	12, soaked and seeded
Lemon grass (serai)	4 stalks, lightly crushed	Fresh red chillies	5
Tamarind pulp (asam Jawa)	1 Tbsp, mixed with 125 ml water and strained	Shallots	12, peeled
		Dried prawn (shrimp) paste (belacan)	2.5 x 2.5 x 1-cm piece
Sweet basil leaves (daun selasih)	8 sprigs	Turmeric (kunyit)	2.5-cm knob, peeled

Method

▌ Season fish with 1 tsp salt, pepper and shallot oil. Place on lightly greased steaming dish.

▌ Separate and reserve outer petals and stems of torch ginger buds. Thinly slice inner buds and set aside.

▌ Heat cooking oil in a wok and lightly brown onion pieces. Add lemon grass, torch ginger bud petals and stems and ground ingredients. Stir-fry over low heat for 5 minutes.

▌ Add tamarind juice and bring to a slow boil. Add basil leaves, sugar and 1 tsp salt. Simmer for 2–3 minutes. Add coconut milk and simmer until thick.

▌ Meanwhile, steam fish over rapidly boiling water for 12 minutes.

▌ Drain liquid off steaming dish, then pour or spoon on tamarind sauce. Serve hot.

steamed fish with sichuan vegetables

Ingredients

Fish	1, 600–700 g, cleaned, use threadfin *(ikan kurau/ senangin)*, sea bass *(ikan siakap)* or tail end of salmon *(ikan salmon)*
Salt	1 tsp
Ground white pepper	1/2 tsp
Shallot oil	1/2 Tbsp
Preserved Sichuan vegetables	150 g (1 1/2 packets), shredded
Chilli oil	3 Tbsp
Shallots	3, peeled and sliced
Garlic	6 cloves, peeled and minced
Young ginger	3-cm knob, peeled and minced
Red chillies	3, 2 chopped and 1 julienned
Chinese rice wine	1 Tbsp
Corn flour (cornstarch)	1 Tbsp, mixed with 2 Tbsp fresh chicken stock or water to make thickener

Sauce (combined)

Fresh chicken stock	250 ml
Sugar	1 1/2 tsp
Oyster sauce	3 tsp
Light soy sauce	2 tsp
Dark soy sauce	2 tsp

Method

❚ Make 2–3 diagonal slits on each side of fish. Season with salt, pepper and shallot oil, then set aside.

❚ Soak Sichuan vegetables in some water for 10 minutes. Drain well before use.

❚ Steam fish over rapidly boiling water for 10–12 minutes or until just cooked.

❚ Heat chilli oil in a saucepan. Lightly brown shallots, garlic and ginger. Add chopped chillies and Sichuan vegetables, then swirl in wine.

❚ Stir in combined sauce ingredients and bring to the boil. Add thickener.

❚ Remove fish from steamer. Drain liquid from steaming dish into thickened vegetable sauce and mix well.

❚ Pour sauce over steamed fish, garnish with remaining chilli and serve hot.

Note: For Muslims, the Chinese rice wine in this recipe can be omitted without seriously affecting the overall taste of the dish.

steamed fish with dried tangerine peel

Ingredients

Whole fish	1, about 600 g, use spotted red grouper *(ikan kerapu sonoh)*, grouper *(ikan kerapu)*, threadfin *(ikan kurau/ senangin)* or sea bass *(ikan siakap)*
Dried tangerine peel	¼ piece, about 2 g, soaked for 20 minutes or until softened
Sugar	¼ tsp
Shallot or cooking oil	½ tsp
Young ginger	4 slices, peeled and finely shredded
Red chilli	½, seeded and finely shredded
Spring onion (scallion)	1, cut into 3-cm lengths and finely shredded
Red chilli	1, seeded and julienned

Seasoning

Salt	½ tsp
Potato flour	1 tsp
Ground white pepper	½ tsp
Shallot or cooking oil	½ Tbsp

Sauce (combined)

Fresh chicken stock	2 Tbsp
Light soy sauce	1½ Tbsp
Dark soy sauce	½ Tbsp
Sugar	1 tsp
Ground white pepper	a dash

Method

| Make 2 diagonal slits on each side of cleaned fish. Rub on seasoning ingredients and leave for 15 minutes.

| Remove pith of tangerine peel by lightly scraping with a teaspoon. Then, rinse and shred into thin strips. Put shreds into a small bowl and mix with sugar and shallot or cooking oil.

| Place seasoned fish onto a heatproof (flameproof) oval dish. Top with tangerine peel, ginger and chilli.

| Steam over high heat for 12–15 minutes, depending on thickness of fish.

| Meanwhile, place combined sauce ingredients in a small saucepan and heat until just bubbling. Mix in spring onion and chilli; reserve some for garnishing if desired.

| Pour hot sauce over fish and serve.

steamed fish head with bird's eye chilli and ginger paste

Ingredients

Fish head	1/2, large, 750–800 g, use *song* fish *(ikan tongsan kepala besar)*, red snapper *(ikan merah)* or grouper *(ikan kerapu)*		
		Chicken stock	150 ml
		Chinese cooking wine *(hua tiao)*	1 Tbsp
Young ginger	175 g, peeled and finely minced	Sesame oil	1 tsp
Water	1 litre		
Shallot or cooking oil	2 Tbsp	**Seasoning**	
Garlic	4 cloves, peeled and finely minced	Salt	1 tsp
		Ground white pepper	1/2 tsp
Bird's eye chillies *(cili padi)*	10, seeded and chopped	Shallot or cooking oil	1/2 Tbsp
Salted whole soy bean sauce	2 tsp, drained	**Garnishing**	
Spring onions (scallions)	5, white parts only, finely chopped	Coriander leaves (cilantro)	
Sugar	1 1/2 tsp	Spring onion (scallion)	
Salt	1 tsp		

Method

▌ Rub fish head with seasoning ingredients and set aside for 15 minutes.

▌ Put minced ginger into a small saucepan and add half the water. Bring to the boil and leave to simmer for 1–2 minutes. Strain ginger and discard liquid.

▌ Repeat boiling ginger with remaining water. After straining, press out as much excess liquid as possible from ginger pulp and set aside.

▌ Heat oil in a wok and stir-fry prepared ginger for 3–4 minutes or until fragrant.

▌ Add garlic, chillies and soy beans. Stir-fry for 2 minutes more or until lightly browned.

▌ Add spring onions and stir in sugar and salt. Cook for 1 minute before adding stock. Bring to the boil, reduce heat and simmer for 2–3 minutes or until mixture is slightly thickened.

▌ Lastly, stir in wine and sesame oil. Remove from heat and let mixture cool.

▌ Spread cooled mixture onto fish head, then steam over rapidly boiling water for 15 minutes.

▌ Garnish as desired and serve hot.

Note: The song *fish or* soong yee *in Cantonese is a local freshwater carp valued for the thick, smooth flesh surrounding its head. Steaming is one of the best ways to savour its flavour and texture. For Muslims, the Chinese cooking wine in this recipe can be omitted without seriously affecting the overall taste of the dish.*

steamed pomfret with turkey ham and mushrooms

Ingredients

Pomfret	1, 600–700 g, use Chinese (ikan bawal tambak) or white (ikan bawal putih) varieties		
Salt	1 tsp		
Light soy sauce	1 tsp	Young ginger	5 slices, peeled and shredded
Chinese rice wine	1 Tbsp		
Sesame oil	1 tsp	Cooking oil	2 Tbsp
Turkey ham	2 slices, cut into 4-cm squares	Sesame oil	1 tsp
Ginger	4 slices, peeled and halved, for stuffing	Spring onions (scallions)	2, cut into 4-cm lengths
Dried Chinese mushrooms	3, soaked to soften, stems discarded and halved	Coriander leaves (cilantro)	2 sprigs, cut into 4-cm lengths
		Tomato	1, sliced

Method

▌ Clean fish and make 4 diagonal cuts down to the bone. Season fish with salt, light soy sauce, rice wine and sesame oil. Set aside for 30 minutes.

▌ Stuff each cut with ham and ginger slices and mushroom halves. Transfer to steaming dish.

▌ Sprinkle shredded ginger and both oils over fish.

▌ Steam over rapidly boiling water for 15 minutes.

▌ To serve, sprinkle spring onions and coriander leaves over fish and arrange tomato slices around dish. Serve hot.

Note: For Muslims, the Chinese rice wine in this recipe can be omitted without seriously affecting the overall taste of the dish.

stir- &
pan-fried

fried fish with hot soy bean garlic sauce

Ingredients

Yellowtails (*ikan delah*) or chubb mackerels (*ikan kembung*)	6, medium-sized		
Salt	1 tsp	Red chillies	5, seeded and sliced
Ground white pepper	1/4 tsp	Bird's eye chillies (*cili padi*)	6, seeded and chopped
Cooking oil	5 Tbsp	Hot garlic soy bean paste	3 Tbsp
Cooking oil	3 Tbsp		
Onion	1, peeled and sliced	Water	90 ml
Shallots	5, peeled and coarsely pounded	Sugar	1 tsp
		Spring onions (scallions)	2, cut diagonally into 1-cm pieces
Garlic	2 cloves, peeled and coarsely pounded		

Method

▌ Season fish with salt and pepper. Set aside for 15 minutes.

▌ Heat 5 Tbsp oil in a deep saucepan. Fry fish on both sides until golden brown and cooked through. Drain and place on a serving dish.

▌ Heat 3 Tbsp oil in a clean saucepan and fry onion slices until soft.

▌ Add shallots and garlic and cook for 1 minute. Add chillies and soy bean paste. Stir-fry over low heat for 1 minute more or until fragrant.

▌ Add water and bring to the boil. Stir in sugar and simmer for 1 minute or until liquid thickens slightly.

▌ Pour gravy over fried fish. Garnish with spring onions and serve.

fish with spicy plum sauce

Ingredients

Grouper (ikan kerapu) fillet	600 g
Cooking oil	5 Tbsp
Ginger	5-cm knob, peeled and chopped
Garlic	4 cloves, peeled and minced
Plum sauce	1 Tbsp
Coriander leaves (cilantro)	2 sprigs, chopped
Spring onions (scallions)	2, chopped
Red chilli	1, seeded and chopped

Sauce (combined)

Light soy sauce	2 tsp
Dark soy sauce	2 tsp
Chilli sauce	2 tsp
Sugar	2 tsp
Salt	1 tsp

Method

▮ Cut fish fillet into 2 x 3-cm pieces. Set aside.

▮ Heat oil in a wok. Add fish and fry for 1 minute or until nearly cooked. Remove and drain.

▮ Scoop out excess oil, leaving about 2 Tbsp in wok. Brown ginger and garlic.

▮ Return fish to wok and stir-fry. Add combined sauce ingredients and stir-fry carefully until fish is cooked through.

▮ Add remaining ingredients and mix well. Dish out and serve hot.

stir- & pan-fried

fish and herb rice

Ingredients

Salmon (ikan salmon) or grouper (ikan kerapu) fillet	200 g, cut into small dice
Salt	$1/2$ tsp
Freshly ground black pepper	a few grinds
Calrose rice	360 g (2 rice cups), washed and drained well
Water	525 ml (3 rice cups)
Butter or margarine	1 Tbsp
Onions	2, peeled and diced
Garlic	2 cloves, peeled and chopped
Butter or margarine	1 Tbsp
Green capsicum (bell pepper)	1, large, cut into 1-cm dice
Tomatoes	2, large, cut into 1-cm dice
Salt	$1^1/2$ tsp
Chicken stock	85 ml
Ground white pepper	$1/2$ tsp
Italian salad dressing	2 tsp
Chopped parsley	1 Tbsp

Garnishing

Chopped spring onion (scallion)
Chopped coriander leaves (cilantro)
Red chilli (optional)

Method

▌ Season fish with $1/2$ tsp salt and black pepper. Set aside.

▌ Combine washed rice and water in an electric rice cooker and set to cook. Later, loosen cooled, cooked rice and set aside.

▌ Heat 1 Tbsp butter or margarine and stir-fry fish until just cooked. Drain and set aside.

▌ Fry onions and garlic in remaining butter or margarine until soft. Add green pepper and tomatoes; reserve some for extra garnishing if desired . Cook until tender.

▌ Stir in cooked rice and mix well. Add $1^1/2$ tsp salt, chicken stock, white pepper, salad dressing, parsley and cooked fish.

▌ Heat through, then dish out, garnish as desired and serve.

fish with mango sambal

Ingredients

Whole fish	1, 600–700 g, cleaned, use threadfin trevally (ikan cermin), white pomfret (ikan bawal putih) or sea bass (ikan siakap)
Cooking oil	5 Tbsp
Tomato	1, ripe, finely chopped
Anchovy (ikan bilis) or chicken stock	100 ml, or water
Mango	1, half-ripe, about 300 g, peeled, seeded and cut into 0.5-cm thick strips

Seasoning

Kalamansi lime (limau kesturi) juice	extracted from 1 lime
Salt	1 tsp

Ground white pepper	1/4 tsp

Ingredients to be ground (processed)

Red chillies	8, seeded
Garlic	3 cloves, peeled
Shallots	8, peeled
Dried prawn (shrimp) paste (belacan) granules	1 rounded (heaped) tsp
Salt	1 tsp
Sugar	1/2 tsp

Method

I Make 2 diagonal slits on each side of fish. Rub fish all over with seasoning ingredients. Set aside for 15 minutes.

I Heat oil in a wok. Shallow-fry fish on both sides until golden and cooked through. Drain and place on serving dish. Strain and reserve remaining oil.

I Heat 3 Tbsp strained oil in a clean wok. Fry ground ingredients over low heat until fragrant and oil separates.

I Stir in tomato and cook for 1 minute. Add stock or water and bring to the boil.

I Add mango strips and simmer for 3 minutes or until sauce thickens.

I Pour hot sauce over fish. Serve with rice.

stingray dry curry

Ingredients

Stingray *(ikan pari)* or lemon sole	1.5–2 kg, cut into 3.5-cm cubes	Skinned black lentils or gram *(urad dhal)*	2 rounded (heaped) tsp
Ground chilli	3 Tbsp	Fenugreek seeds *(halba)*	1¹/₂ tsp
Ground turmeric *(kunyit serbuk)*	2 tsp	Onion	1, large, peeled, halved and sliced
Ground cumin *(jintan putih serbuk)*	2 tsp	Peeled garlic	80 g, sliced
Tamarind pulp *(asam Jawa)*	25 g, mixed with 250 ml water and strained	Curry leaves	4 sprigs, stems discarded
Salt	2¹/₂ tsp	Fresh chicken stock or water	190 ml
Cooking oil	3 Tbsp	Red chilli	1, for garnishing

Method

▌ Put fish pieces into a large mixing bowl and set aside.

▌ Mix together ground chilli, turmeric and cumin. Set aside.

▌ Blend tamarind juice with salt and mixed spices until smooth, then pour mixture over fish and leave for at least 1 hour.

▌ Heat oil in a wok and fry lentils until golden brown. Add fenugreek and fry until light brown.

▌ Add onion and garlic and fry until onion slices are limp. Add curry leaves and sauté until fragrant. Reserve a few leaves for garnishing if desired.

▌ Pour in fish pieces and marinade, then add stock or water. Cover and cook over high heat, stirring occasionally, until fish is cooked and gravy thick.

▌ Garnish and serve with rice.

stir-fried fish with chilli bean sauce

This is a dish of tantalisingly crisp fish soaked in the wonderful flavours of a delightful spicy bean sauce.

Ingredients

Skinned fish fillets	450 g, cut into 5 x 2.5-cm pieces, use grouper (ikan kerapu), red snapper (ikan merah) or any firm white-fleshed fish	Chilli bean sauce	1 Tbsp
		Spring onions (scallions)	3, cut diagonally into 5-cm lengths
Salt	1 tsp	Potato starch flour	1 tsp, mixed with 1 Tbsp fresh chicken stock or water to make thickener
Ground white pepper	1/4 tsp		
Cooking oil for deep-frying			
Potato starch flour for coating		**Sauce (combined)**	
Cooking oil	1 Tbsp	Fresh chicken stock	200 ml
Finely chopped garlic	1 Tbsp	Dark soy sauce	1 tsp
Finely chopped young ginger	1/2 Tbsp	Chinese cooking wine (hua tiao)	2 Tbsp, or dry sherry
Salted whole soy bean sauce	1 tsp	Sesame oil	2 tsp
		Sugar	2 tsp
		Salt	1/2 tsp
		Ground white pepper	1/4 tsp

Method

1. Season fish pieces with salt and pepper and leave for 15 minutes.
1. Heat sufficient oil for deep-frying in a medium-sized saucepan. Coat fish with potato starch flour, then lower in to cook until golden brown. Drain and place on paper towels.
1. Heat 1 Tbsp oil in a clean wok. Lightly brown garlic and ginger. Add whole and chilli bean sauces and stir-fry for 10 seconds.
1. Pour in combined sauce ingredients and bring to the boil.
1. Return fish to wok and add spring onions; reserve some for garnishing if desired. Carefully stir-fry for 1–2 minutes, then add thickener.
1. When gravy is thickened, dish out and serve hot with rice.

stir-fried chilli fish

Ingredients

Fish fillet	250 g, sliced or diced, use grouper *(ikan kerapu)* or threadfin *(ikan kurau/ senangin)*		

Seasoning

Light soy sauce	1 tsp
Oyster sauce	1 tsp
Ginger juice	1 tsp
Salt	a pinch
Water	1 Tbsp
Corn flour (cornstarch)	1 tsp

Shallot or corn oil	1 Tbsp
Garlic	2 cloves, peeled and minced
Dried chillies	3, rinsed and each cut into 3 sections

Method

▌ Season fish pieces with seasoning ingredients. Set aside for at least 15 minutes.

▌ Heat shallot or corn oil in a wok. Lightly brown garlic, then add chillies and toss for 30 seconds.

▌ Add fish pieces and stir-fry for 5–6 minutes or until just cooked.

stir-fried garlic fish

Ingredients

Fish fillet	250 g, diced, use grouper (*ikan kerapu*), threadfin (*ikan kurau/senangin*) or salmon (*ikan salmon*)
Shallot or corn oil	1 Tbsp
Garlic	6 cloves, peeled and sliced

Seasoning

Light soy sauce	³/₄ Tbsp		
Crushed black peppercorns	1 tsp		
Five-spice powder	¹/₄ tsp		
Sugar	¹/₄ tsp		
Dark soy sauce	¹/₄ tsp		
Corn flour (cornstarch)	1 tsp		
Chilli oil (optional)	¹/₂ Tbsp		

Method

❚ Season fish with seasoning ingredients. Leave for at least 15 minutes.

❚ Heat oil in a frying pan (skillet) and lightly brown garlic.

❚ Add seasoned fish and stir-fry over high heat for 5–6 minutes or until just cooked.

stir-fried fish with sweet peas and leek

Ingredients

Fish fillets	450–500 g, use sole (*ikan lidah/sebelah*) or grouper (*ikan kerapu*)
Cooking oil for deep-frying	
Cooking oil	1 Tbsp
Ginger	3 slices
Shallots	2, peeled and sliced
Garlic	3 cloves, peeled and chopped
Leek	1, small, diagonally sliced
Red chilli	1, seeded and diagonally sliced
Chinese cooking wine (*hua tiao*)	2 tsp
Sweet peas	150 g
Corn flour (cornstarch)	1 1/2 tsp, mixed with 2 Tbsp water to make thickener

Seasoning

Ginger juice	2 tsp
Salt	1/2 tsp
Sugar	1/2 tsp
Ground white pepper	1/4 tsp
Chinese cooking wine (*hua tiao*)	2 tsp
Corn flour (cornstarch)	1 1/2 tsp
Egg white	1/2, lightly beaten

Sauce (combined)

Oyster sauce	1 Tbsp
Light soy sauce	2 tsp
Sugar	1/2 tsp
Chinese cooking wine (*hua tiao*)	2 tsp
Chicken stock	4 Tbsp

Method

I Halve fish fillet, then cut at an angle into 2.5 x 3.5-cm pieces, each 0.75-cm thick. Season with seasoning ingredients, then leave for at least 30 minutes.

I Heat sufficient oil for deep-frying and cook fish for 15 seconds. Drain and place on absorbent paper towels.

I Heat 1 Tbsp oil in a clean wok. Add ginger, shallots and garlic. Stir-fry for a few seconds. Add leek and chilli and toss for 1 minute.

I Return fish to wok and splash in wine. Add sweet peas and stir carefully to avoid breaking fish pieces.

I Pour in combined sauce ingredients and bring to the boil, then add thickener.

I Dish out and serve.

Note: For variation, this dish can also be prepared with threadfin (ikan kurau/senangin) or song fish (ikan tongsan besar). For Muslims, the Chinese cooking wine in this recipe can be omitted without seriously affecting on the overall taste of the dish.

teriyaki fish

Ingredients

Cod *(ikan cod)* fillets	4, each cut into 5 x 8-cm pieces
Cooking oil	2 Tbsp
Cooking oil	1/2 Tbsp
Potato flour	1/2 Tbsp
Dark soy sauce	1/2 tsp
Chopped spring onion (scallion)	1 Tbsp
Chinese lettuce *(sang choy)* for garnishing (optional)	

Marinade (combined)

Lemon juice	1 1/2 Tbsp
Teriyaki sauce	4 Tbsp
Salt	1 tsp
Ground white pepper	1/2 tsp
Garlic	3 cloves, peeled
Grated young ginger	1 tsp
Fresh pineapple or orange juice	190 ml
Sugar	1 1/2 Tbsp

Method

▌ Marinate fish pieces for at least 1 hour, turning over once or twice.

▌ Heat 2 Tbsp oil in a frying pan (skillet). Drain fish from marinade and fry for 1 minute on each side or until just cooked. Remove to a bed of lettuce if using and set aside.

▌ Heat 1/2 Tbsp oil in a clean saucepan.

▌ Stir potato flour and soy sauce into marinade, then pour into heated saucepan. Bring to the boil, stirring constantly until liquid thickens. Stir in spring onion; reserve some for garnishing if desired.

▌ Pour sauce over fish and garnish. Serve hot with rice.

tuna, mushroom and black olive tagliatelle

Ingredients

Olive oil	2 Tbsp		
Garlic	3 cloves, peeled and finely chopped		
Red chilli	1, seeded and chopped		
Anchovies (*ikan bilis*)	2, cleaned		
Oyster mushrooms	120 g, sliced	Fresh chopped basil	1 Tbsp, or 1 tsp dried
Canned tomatoes	1 can (411 g), chopped, preferably of Hunt's brand	Canned tuna (*ikan tongkol*) in oil	1 can (180 g), drained
		Pitted black olives	50 g
Tomato purée	2 Tbsp	Chopped chives	1 Tbsp
Salt	1 tsp	Chopped fresh parsley	3 Tbsp, more for garnishing
Sugar	1 tsp		
Ground white pepper	$^1/_2$ tsp	Tagliatelle	250 g

Method

▌ Heat olive oil in a saucepan. Add garlic and chilli and fry for 1 minute, then stir in anchovies, mushrooms, canned tomatoes and tomato purée. Mix well and allow to cook gently for 5–8 minutes or until sauce thickens.

▌ Stir in salt, sugar, pepper, basil, tuna and olives. Lastly, stir in chives and parsley; reserve some for garnishing if desired. Remove from heat.

▌ Cook tagliatelle according to packet instructions. Drain, portion and transfer noodles to serving plates. Ladle tuna sauce over and serve.

stir-fried dace with chrysanthemum leaves

Ingredients

Dace with salted black beans	1 can (184 g)
Chrysanthemum leaves (tong ho)	500 g, short-stemmed variety preferred
Garlic	2 cloves, peeled and sliced
Sugar	$1/_2$ tsp
Light soy sauce	1 Tbsp

Method

❚ Drain and reserve oil from canned dace. Break fish into rough chunks with a fork and spoon. Set aside.

❚ Discard root ends and hard stems of vegetables. Wash and drain.

❚ Heat a wok with 2 Tbsp reserved oil and lightly brown garlic. Add fish and black beans. Fry for 15 seconds or until fragrant.

❚ Add vegetables, cover wok and allow to cook over high heat for 1 minute.

❚ Remove cover to add sugar and soy sauce. Stir-fry briefly until vegetables are just limp. Dish out and serve with rice.

Note: Canned dace with salted black beans is a quick store-cupboard item commonly steamed plain and eaten with porridge. It is also popular fried with bitter gourd. Fried with chrysanthemum leaves, it takes on a wonderful aroma and will entice you to eat more rice. Drip dry the vegetables well and cook over high heat as the leaves turn watery when cooked.

glossary of ingredients

Bird's eye chillies
Bird's eye chillies are tiny but fiery relatives of chillies. Their size belies the punch packed in the white specks that are their seeds. For a less fiery taste, deseed them or use them whole. If deseeding, handle them with care, ideally with plastic gloves, and be mindful not to rub areas around the eyes.

Chillies
Red chillies may appear more potent than green chillies, but their stinging qualities are probably near equal, and relatively mild. Red chillies contain a certain fruit-like sweetness that is lacking in green chillies, which comparatively taste more like raw vegetables.

Coriander leaves
Also known as cilantro or Chinese parsley, coriander leaves are pungently fragrant. Do not confuse coriander leaves with Chinese celery, which looks very similar, but has thicker, juicier stems and larger leaves. While similarly pungent, Chinese celery tastes completely different from coriander.

Curry leaves
As their name implies, curry leaves impart a distinctly curried fragrance and taste slightly peppery. It is obvious enough to use them in curried dishes for that added lift in aroma and taste. Curry leaves, however, have also been creatively used in dishes of other cuisines to an intriguingly pleasant effect.

Dried sour fruit
This ingredient has no common English name and is frequently mislabelled as "tamarind pieces" by suppliers. "Dried sour fruit" is a direct translation of its Malay name, *asam gelugur*. Usually sold in the form of wrinkled, brown slices, dried sour fruit is a souring agent, much like tamarind pulp, but the fruit itself is completely unrelated to the tamarind family. Also unlike tamarind, dried sour fruit slices are only suited to liquid-based dishes. They are added whole and cooked in liquid until the desired sourness is achieved. After which, they are removed and discarded.

Kaffir lime leaves
The way kaffir lime leaves grow on branches has led to their nickname of "double-lime leaves". Their Malay name is *daun limau purut*. If bought with branches still attached, remove leaves carefully because the branches are dotted with vicious thorns. A pair of scissors is recommended for the task. Kaffir lime leaves are usually either shredded or used whole, but bruised to release their fragrance.

Lady's fingers

Lady's fingers or okra are filled with tiny white balls for seeds, which provide a delightful crunch to the dish to which they have been added. However, lady's fingers also cannot stand to be overcooked and when they have been, release a clear and slimy substance that is, while tasteless, most unsightly.

Lemon grass

Stalks of lemon grass are a creamy pale yellow with green leaves on top. Only the bulbous, lower half of each stalk is used in cooking. The root end and leafy, top half are cut off and discarded. Prepared lemon grass stalks can be added whole after bruising with the handle of a knife or minced.

Palm sugar

These hard, cylindrical blocks of sugar are better known as *gula Melaka* in Singapore and Malaysia. *Gula Melaka* literally translates into "sugar of Melaka" and is made from the sap of certain native varieties of palms. For that reason, palm sugar originating from different parts of Asia contain slight variations in aroma, taste and colour. In Indonesia, it is called *gula Jawa*, or "sugar of Java" and jaggery or *gur* in India.

Pointed pepper leaves

Sometimes called "wild pepper leaves", pointed pepper leaves have a muted bite and serve well as an alternative to green, leafy vegetables. They are, however, more often used as a herb or flavouring agent in cooking. Some Asian cuisines serve extremely fresh pointed pepper leaves raw.

Polygonum leaves

Also known as Vietnamese mint, or *daun kesum* to Malay-speakers, polygonum leaves have a pungent flavour and should be used judiciously, if not sparingly. The richly herby taste of these leaves generally go well with other strong-tasting ingredients. A case in point is *laksa lemak*, a dish of thick rice noodles bathed in a spicy, dense, coconut milk-based soup. Here, shredded polygonum leaves are added as a garnish and make an impressive foil against the richness of the coconut milk.

Torch ginger bud

Pretty pink flowers of the torch ginger plant are deeply aromatic when harvested before they bloom. The entire flower — from the reddish-pink, outer petals to the creamy inner bud and stem — can be used in cooking. The petals, bud and stem are usually separated and used at different stages of cooking.

glossary of fish

Carp
The freshwater or common carp (*Cyprinus carpio*) (illusatrated) is an inexpensive and nutritious fish. Protein-rich and low in fat, the carp is easily identified by the barbels (whisker-like extensions) on the corners of its mouth. The grass or Chinese carp (*Ctenopharyngodon idellus*) and *song* fish (*Aristichthys nobilis*) are other varieties of carp mentioned in this book. Malay-speakers generally call carp *ikan tongsan*.

Grouper
Grouper recipes in this book do not specify which kinds to use because it is mostly a question of personal preferences. The more commonly used ones include red grouper *(Variola louti)*, or *ikan kerapu merah* in Malay; spotted red grouper *(Plectropomus maculatus)*, or *ikan kerapu sonoh*; and flower grouper *(Epinephilus areolatus)* (illustrated), or *ikan kerapu ekor putih*. Red grouper is sometimes also known as moontail grouper.

Mackerel
Three types of mackerels are used in this book. They are chubb or Indian mackerel (*Rastrelliger kanagurta*), or *ikan kembung* in Malay; Spanish mackerel (*Scomberomorus guttatus*) (illustrated, top), or *ikan tenggiri*; and barred Spanish mackerel (*Scomberomorus commersonii*) (illustrated, bottom), or *ikan tenggiri batang*. Despite its name, the horse mackerel (*Caranx sexfasciatus*), or *ikan cupak/bentong*, is unrelated to the mackerel family.

Cod
The Atlantic polar cod (*Gadoid spp.*) is the most sought after, and hence the most valuable, fish for tables the world over. Its white meat is firm, flaky and flavourful. Its less famous relatives, the blue-eyed cod (*Hyperglyche antartica*) (illustrated) and coral cod (*Cephalopholis miniata*) are also favoured for their firm white flesh. The blue-eyed cod is true to its name, while the coral cod is readily identified — orange-red skin with blue spots all over its head and body.

Hilsa
Sometimes referred to as shad, the hilsa (*Hilsa ilisha*) is a remarkably tasty fish but also one full of fine bones, causing it to be unpopular with some adults and unsuitable for younger diners. While its popularity has been steadily waning in some parts of Asia, the hilsa is the single most important fish in Bangladesh, making up one-third of the country's fish production.

Mullet
The mullet or grey mullet (*Mugil dussumierii* or *cephalus*) is known to Malay-speakers as *ikan belanak*. Although rather bony, the mullet compensates with pink and oily flesh that has a distinctive flavour when cooked.

Pomfret

Of the various pomfrets mentioned in this book, the most frequently used are white pomfret (*Pampus argenteus*) (illustrated), or *ikan bawal putih* in Malay; black pomfret (*Formio niger*), or *ikan bawal hitam*; and Chinese pomfret (*Pampus chinensis*), or *ikan bawal tambak*.

Sea bass

Sea bass *(Lates calcarifer)* is a popular food fish, which Malay-speakers know as *ikan siakap*. It is dark along the back and silvery on either side.

Snapper

Snapper recipes in this book call for one of three types: red snapper (*Lutjanus sanguineus*) (illustrated), or *ikan merah* in Malay; mangrove snapper (*Lutjanus argentimaculatus*), or *ikan jenahak*; and golden snapper (*Lutjanus johni*), or *ikan ungar*. Mangrove snapper is sometimes known as mangrove jack.

Sole

A flatfish, sole (*Synaptura commersonii*) is known to Malay-speakers as *ikan lidah/sebelah*. Its flesh is white, fine and delicate-tasting when cooked.

Stingray

Stingray (*Dasyatis zugei*) is known as *ikan pari* in Malay and its wings make a meaty and bone-free alternative to fish steaks. Stingray wings only have a layer of cartilage across their centres which makes for easy filleting. When cooked, the dense meat separates into large flakes.

Threadfin

Threadfin (*Polynemus indicus*), or *ikan kurau* or *senangin* to Malay-speakers, is a tasty fish prized for having few bones. For that reason, it has a reputation for being the ideal fish for toddlers in Singapore and Malaysia.

Trevally

Two varieties of trevally are mentioned in this book. They are golden trevally (*Caranx speciosus*) (illustrated), or *ikan gerong-gerong* in Malay, and threadfin trevally (*Alectis indicus*), or *ikan cermin*.

Tuna

Yellow fin tuna (*Thunnus albacares*) (illustrated, top) and skipjack tuna (*Katsuwonus pelamis*) (illustrated, bottom) are two varieties of tuna commonly found in tropical waters. Malay-speakers generally call tuna *ikan tongkol*.

weights & measures

Quantities for this book are given in Metric and American (spoon and cup) measures. Standard spoon and cup measurements used are: 1 tsp = 5 ml, 1 Tbsp = 15 ml, 1 cup = 250 ml. All measures are level unless otherwise stated.

LIQUID AND VOLUME MEASURES

Metric	Imperial	American
5 ml	1/6 fl oz	1 teaspoon
10 ml	1/3 fl oz	1 dessertspoon
15 ml	1/2 fl oz	1 tablespoon
60 ml	2 fl oz	1/4 cup (4 tablespoons)
85 ml	2 1/2 fl oz	1/3 cup
90 ml	3 fl oz	3/8 cup (6 tablespoons)
125 ml	4 fl oz	1/2 cup
180 ml	6 fl oz	3/4 cup
250 ml	8 fl oz	1 cup
300 ml	10 fl oz (1/2 pint)	1 1/4 cups
375 ml	12 fl oz	1 1/2 cups
435 ml	14 fl oz	1 3/4 cups
500 ml	16 fl oz	2 cups
625 ml	20 fl oz (1 pint)	2 1/2 cups
750 ml	24 fl oz (1 1/5 pints)	3 cups
1 litre	32 fl oz (1 3/5 pints)	4 cups
1.25 litres	40 fl oz (2 pints)	5 cups
1.5 litres	48 fl oz (2 2/5 pints)	6 cups
2.5 litres	80 fl oz (4 pints)	10 cups

DRY MEASURES

Metric	Imperial
30 grams	1 ounce
45 grams	1 1/2 ounces
55 grams	2 ounces
70 grams	2 1/2 ounces
85 grams	3 ounces
100 grams	3 1/2 ounces
110 grams	4 ounces
125 grams	4 1/2 ounces
140 grams	5 ounces
280 grams	10 ounces
450 grams	16 ounces (1 pound)
500 grams	1 pound, 1 1/2 ounces
700 grams	1 1/2 pounds
800 grams	1 3/4 pounds
1 kilogram	2 pounds, 3 ounces
1.5 kilograms	3 pounds, 4 1/2 ounces
2 kilograms	4 pounds, 6 ounces

LENGTH

Metric	Imperial
0.5 cm	1/4 inch
1 cm	1/2 inch
1.5 cm	3/4 inch
2.5 cm	1 inch

OVEN TEMPERATURE

	°C	°F	Gas Regulo
Very slow	120	250	1
Slow	150	300	2
Moderately slow	160	325	3
Moderate	180	350	4
Moderately hot	190/200	370/400	5/6
Hot	210/220	410/440	6/7
Very hot	230	450	8
Super hot	250/290	475/550	9/10

ABBREVIATION

tsp	teaspoon
Tbsp	tablespoon
g	gram
kg	kilogram
ml	millilitre